Hi Kay

this was a 1st Draft
So there are small errors,
but hopefully you will enjoy
Some of the experiences.

Mark.
x x

Prologue: Go West Young Man!

I won't forget the summer of '73, it was my first trip down to the far west of Cornwall, for a fortnight's holiday in St Ives, and to spend time with my my Cornish cousins. We had travelled from Reading, a few miles west of London, on a train pulled by the 'Western Leviathan.' As it rumbled and rolled to a stop alongside our platform, I was in awe. In retrospect, it seems fitting that I first entered Cornwall, a land of giants such as Cormoron, Bolster and Antony Payne, in a living, breathing metal beast, named after a sea monster! A thrilling five hour journey westwards soon followed, and I can still recall the excitement of crossing I. K. Brunel's magnificent railway bridge over the Tamar, heading in to Cornwall, with dad teasing us, saying, "Did you remember to bring your passports?" Up above us to my right, on the road bridge, a large sign read: 'Welcome to Cornwall.' Those words seemed innocuous enough, but they had attitude; I had half-expected to see one of those lightning flashes so beloved of old black and white horror films. It was more than just a road sign, it was a defiant declaration of Cornish independence, it told us that Cornwall was not just another run of the mill English county. Some of the names of the railway stations that we would soon pass in Cornwall would confirm those initial feelings, it had all seemed so exotic to a young lad from rural Surrey; a few stations even had palm trees on the platforms!

As the Western Leviathan sped onwards, further and further westwards in to the Cornish interior, I soon had my first sight of the fabled 'St Austell Mountains,' over to our left, towards the south coast. Dad explained they weren't really mountains, how it was just accumulated waste from an industrial extraction process which had built up over the years, as thousands of trucks had jettisoned their waste, higher and higher up on the ever-growing waste heaps; giving them a greyish mountain-like appearance. As we continued to thunder on down through Cornwall, I had begun to notice, dotted around the bleak furze and heather covered moors, many decrepit tin-mine engine houses, and air-shafts, in various stages of decay; wrapped up in ivy the circumference of ships' ropes. After passing St Austell by, on the approach to the old industrial mining heartlands of Redruth and Camborne, the landscape had begun to look increasingly grim, foreboding, and, well, haunted. This was a strange alien land, but I was already beginning to fall in love with it. The Leviathan's final destination was to be the Great Western Railway's Terminus at Penzance, but we had to get off it ten minutes earlier, at St Erth Railway Station, in order to catch a smaller connecting train along the coast to St Ives.

I had been browsing through a tourist map of Cornwall on the train, and couldn't help but notice the preponderance of mysterious sounding place names in Cornwall. Many had the prefix 'St' for Saint, I'd find out later that it wasn't that the Cornish were particularly holy, but evidence that the village-culture of the invading Saxon tribes hadn't made too much headway that far west. Unfamiliar place names like Marazion, Nanjizel, Perranzabuloe, Praze and Beeble, and Zennor (The Cornish love their Zs) were both musical and magical to my young English ears, and, well, foreign. As D.H. Lawrence once correctly remarked of Cornwall: 'It's not England.'

An announcement, by a very upper crust lady more suited to the Home Counties, came over the train's loud-speaker, "St Erth for St Ives, St Erth for St Ives, passengers wishing to travel to St Ives should alight here for the connection service, the next stop will be St Erth for St Ives." On arrival at St Erth Railway Station I recall dad smiling and reminiscing, he told me that when he was on leave from the RAF (Royal Air Force) in the early 1950s, my Uncle Ken had picked him up from here on his old Triumph motor-bike. He said he had to hold on for dear life, as Ken joyfully smashed through the speed limit on the narrow, twisting, Cornish country lanes, expertly managing to find every possible bump and hole in the road between the railway station and his cottage in Chennalls Lane!

St Erth was a well-kept railway station, with its pretty pansies hanging in pillar box red galvanised G.W.R. (Great Western Railway) buckets, wild buddleias in profusion behind the black gloss painted spiked iron railings, and large primary coloured rail-travel posters encouraging us all to visit York, or perhaps the English Riviera. But we were all happy to be in Cornwall, my dad always felt so at home here, in a landscape he loved, amongst his adoring Cornish family. I recall him stood there on the platform, relaxed, looking around, reaching in to his jacket for his pipe, ruminatively pushing a little bit of 'baccy' in to his pipe bowl with his powerful index finger, and lighting up in that intense, ritualistic way, that pipe smokers did when I was a kid. Mum had soon broken the spell, "Give us a hand Bob!" Our mum was busily rounding us all up, like a shepherdess ensuring her little lambs were all off the train before it rumbled on towards Penzance. We excitedly headed over the footbridge together, with dad, a powerfully built man, then in his prime, taking the lion's share of the bags. He huffed and he puffed, and he didn't complain......well, not that much. We were headed over the main Cornwall to London railway tracks, towards the little branch line platform that is now so familiar to me, breathing in the scents of the Cornish air, a heady blend of the sea, the estuary mudflats, and diesel fumes from the departing Leviathan, to await the most scenic train-journey I've ever taken. The legendary branch line to St Ives.

As the little train left St Erth Railway Station with its happy human cargo, it had wobbled precariously, criss-crossing several railway lines to get on to the right road, it began to hug the muddy riverbank of the Hayle Estuary, then slowly by-passed Lelant Railway Station, with its pretty green station house. A few minutes later, close to where the Hayle Estuary opens out in to the glorious wide expanse of St Ives Bay, the little train meandered around a slow left hand bend, before proceeding on towards our final destination. We were soon to glimpse the bewitching Island at St Ives in the distance, with its diminutive stone chapel perched on the top, like a cherry sits on a bun. The chapel, floating in a morning heat haze, had resembled a magical scene straight out of Arthurian legend. An audible murmur of excitement rippled throughout the train, from children of all ages; three to eighty. Dad had made that trip so many times before, beginning not long after the 1939/45 war, with his parents, but he would never lose that child-like enthusiasm for Cornwall, and St Ives in particular, and neither will I. The train trundled along expectantly, rocking ever so slightly from side to side, as it caressed the attractive, wooded, feminine curves of the beautiful coast-line, briefly stopping to drop off a family of happy, smiley holidaymakers at Carbis Bay, and then, after just one more wooded headland for the driver to negotiate, we had finally rolled in to St Ives, weary, but excited for the fun that we all knew was to come.

We alighted there, in to that famous light I'd heard so much about, which had called and inspired so many creatives to the little town down through the years, from Olsson and Berlin, to Donovan and Hepworth. We were met there, on the solitary platform, by my dad's two diminutive, lovable Cornish cousins, who had driven down the Stennack, and through the busy little town to greet us in their blue Triumph Dolomite. My Aunty Joyce, and her sister Mary, of ancient Cornish stock, were two of the sweetest, kindest ladies I have ever met. That day was to be the beginning of my Cornish love affair, it's now forty-six years later, and sadly they have now both passed on, but my love for them, my extended Cornish family, and St Ives, remains as strong as ever. Indeed, my passion for the far west of Cornwall has grown ever deeper by the year, as I continue to learn more about her mysteries, history, legends, folklore and culture.

The Western Leviathan, aptly named after a sea monster!

Mark Anthony Wyatt

The Spirit of Cornwall:

A Haunted Legacy

Volume One

Foreword by Michael Williams, paranormal researcher, investigator, author and Cornish Bard.

Based on interviews and research carried out by
Mark Anthony Wyatt, between 2016 and 2019.

Excerpts taken from Michael Williams' work were done so with his permission.

Leviathan Media Productions
©

Disclaimer

Every effort was made to trace copyright holders, in order to obtain their permission to use copyrighted material. I gratefully acknowledge everybody who has, in any way at all, contributed to this book.

Published By *Leviathan Media Productions.*

Cover Design: Mark Anthony Wyatt and Janice Louise Maier.

Editor: Grammar Nazi Services LLC.

Grammar: Before we begin on volume one, here are just a few words on my use of grammar, for anybody that might care about such things….but, if you don't, please move on to something more interesting in the book, I know I probably would!

I have combined American-English grammar and punctuation rules with English grammar and punctuation rules. I'm English, but I now spend a lot of time in the U.S., and I probably have a lot more readers in the States, so a compromise seemed only natural. However, I did draw the line at removing the letter 'U' from words like 'colour,' and despite 'spell-check' always insisting on 'traveling,' I will always spell it with two 'L's. But, overall, I believe that consistency is the key. So, if you are English, and you think that I have made a grammar or punctuation mistake (and I may well have done) the likelihood is that I'm just using American-English grammar and punctuation, and, of course, the opposite applies too, So I've covered my ****!

Dedication to Michael Williams

This first volume of 'The Spirit of Cornwall: A Haunted Legacy' is dedicated to the memory of Michael Williams, 1933-2019: a highly esteemed author and journalist, a specialist on topics as diverse as the supernatural, culture and sport. Michael was also an investigative researcher; publisher; private school-master; and an animal welfare benefactor and reformer. He enjoyed the theatre and was a voracious reader, he had an impressive library in his study on the edge of Bodmin Moor. Michael loved all sports, but cricket and rugby in particular, indeed, he was the founder of the Cornish Crusaders Cricket Club, and one of the early leading lights of the Penzance Pirates Rugby Club. He was elected as a member of the prestigious Ghost Club in London, alongside his old friend Peter Underwood, the famous British ghost hunter and author. Michael was a genuine, kind, polite Cornish gentleman, with perfect manners. He was rightfully acknowledged by the Gorsedh Kernow in 1997, when he was awarded a Bardship for his meritorious work for Cornish culture. His Bardic title, 'Gwaryer lyes-tu' is very apt, it is Cornish for 'All-Rounder.' Michael is sorely missed by all who had the honour and pleasure to have known him.

Michael Williams

1933-2019

"Back in time, Irish and Breton blood flowed into my Cornish family tree; little wonder then that I feel distinctly Celtic, fervently believing that Cornwall is not just another English county, but a people and a place apart!"

Michael Williams, speaking in 1973.

Table of Contents

Foreword

Mark and I first met through our mutual membership of Paranormal Investigation, an exclusive group that I set up back in the 1960s, to explore the edges of the unknown in the south-west of England, but particularly so in Cornwall.

It was the Reverend Sabine Baring-Gould, the legendary Squire of Lewtrenchard, who first set me out on my own supernatural journey. Among many mysterious topics and legends, I spent many years researching the Lost Land of Lyonesse, which was said to have laid between the extreme west of Penwith and the Isles of Scilly. There have been so many sightings of fragments from Lyonesse, witnessed by Cornish fishermen in clear water on fine days. We have our Mermaids too, but in Cornwall we like to call them Merry Maids. Charles Causley, the author of 'The Water-Babies,' wrote about a remarkable Merry Maid at Zennor on the North Cornish coast.

I am pleased that Mark is devoting time and energy to researching the granite connection to anomalous activities and creativity, particularly so down here in Cornwall, where there is undoubtedly an abundance of all three. Cornwall is granite country, it has a character which somehow lifts morale. In the halcyon days of the Rugby County Championship, as a sports journalist on the Cornish Guardian, I would occasionally write about 'granite forwards,' robust men like Bonzo Johns and Stack Stevens. There was an awesome power about those rugged, proud, competitive Cornish men, and it somehow personified the very spirit of Trelawny. The Rev R.S. Hawker, in his poem, 'The Song of the Western Men,' posed the question, 'and shall Trelawny die?' No, it won't, not as long as we have Cornish men and women of their calibre!

A quick peek at my desk calendar reveals that Cornwall retains a healthy calendar of unique festivals and customs, which we must retain; they make us a people and place apart. Above all, I hope you will enjoy these amazing experiences that Mark has collated, researched, and presented to you for your interest and enjoyment

Michael Williams
Wadebridge
Cornwall
February, 2019

(Sadly, Michael, my friend and writing mentor, passed away on the 31st March of this year, 2019, just a few weeks after kindly writing my Foreword.)

Introduction

For most people who know of it, but don't actually live here, Cornwall is likely just another English county. They'll know of Cornwall as a region of beautiful Mediterranean-like sandy beaches; quaint seaside fishing villages; sun-bronzed surfers; the dramatic locations for popular TV series such as Poldark and Doc Martin, and, of course, they will probably have heard about our delicious Cornish cream teas too! However, leaving aside for now the rather contentious idea that Cornwall is in any way English, there's also a lesser known, more mysterious, unworldly, darker side to Cornwall, of which they may not yet be aware. For those who are prepared to look though, Cornwall does have an abundance of strange tales about Mermaids; Knockers; Piskies; Spriggans; Giants; Owl Men; wizards; sea monsters; Bucca; big cats and hounds; phantom trains, planes, automobiles, ships and bicycles; UFOs; all manner of ghosts, and other 'head-scratchers' (Jim Harold's term) of all kinds too! I hope you will enjoy exploring these witness experiences, with me going on ahead as your guide, holding a Cornish Davy miner's safety lamp aloft, lighting up our narrow gorse enclosed tracks, across our high, misty Cornish moors; and hopefully we'll see any Spriggans before they see us! No other region of Britain packs such a diverse range of mysteries, history, legends, creativity and folklore in to such a small area. Paranormally, and creatively speaking, Cornwall has always punched well above her weight, perhaps that has something to do with the abundant presence of granite here, which I will discuss in more detail in volume two. Cornwall's anomalous activities are very much distinctive to her independent national identity, traditions, customs, superstitions and culture.

If you are fascinated by the supernatural, and you love Cornwall, then you're in the right place here! I'm hopeful you will enjoy these two volumes, they are wide-ranging and ambitious in their scope; they're not just another collection of ghost and UFO stories randomly thrown together. The supernatural is like ivy that twists and turns around this ancient granite Cornish kingdom, as the following strange witness experiences will soon reveal. I have tried to paint you a vivid picture with my chosen words, so that even if you haven't yet travelled here, you may still, hopefully, feel something of our unique Cornish atmosphere seeping through the pages in to your fingers, or perhaps metaphorically oozing out of your screen! Wherever possible, I have tried to match my witnesses' experiences up to interesting background information, and known historical events, as they may well have had some bearing on their strange encounters, and I've also tried to show some possible links between old and new Cornish folklore, and modern Ufology.

In this first volume, we'll be in the eastern half of Cornwall visiting some fascinating Cornish locations, including a top secret government spy base on a remote North Cornish cliff-top, an abandoned military airfield high up on Bodmin Moor, and some haunted pubs, cafes and churches. I will be discussing several colourful characters, people such as Antony Payne, the Stratton Giant; Robert Stephen Hawker, the eccentric vicar of Morwenstow; Prudence Pepper, an ex-London Blitz ambulance driver and motor-biker; and Daphne Du Maurier, the acclaimed novelist. In this volume, and the second, you'll read of how the British military regularly pursues UFOs in Cornish air space, and of the latest, cutting-edge, technical developments in paranormal research. I'll also be discussing how modern quantum science relates to the supernatural, and I'll frequently be musing on the true nature of reality and consciousness. There will be some poltergeist activity too, strange orb lights, and tales of a legendary sunken land off the far western Cornish coast. We'll also be discussing the customs and superstitions of Cornish tin miners, and how Cornish folklore 'emigrated' to the U.S., and other parts of the world, alongside Cornish miners.

Dive in with me then, like one of our Cornish Merry Maids, let's go deeper together than a Peter Benchley novel, in to an abyss of unfathomable Cornish mysteries, history, legends, creativity and folklore. I have mostly avoided the better known, more frequently told Cornish mysteries, in order to explore some interesting, never before published witness accounts, and to tell you some lesser told stories that I feel deserve to be heard again. Each chapter is very different to the others in the book, so please feel free to jump around at random if you wish, some chapters are (necessarily) quite long, and others are quite brief, but I'm confident that you will find plenty to hold your interest in all of them. A few of these witness experiences, in both volumes, were my own, so if you enjoy reading about them, please also seek out my first book, 'Wyatt's Weird World,' and the second volume of 'The Spirit of Cornwall: A Haunted Legacy,' which are both available on-line at Amazon, and from Waterstones, Barnes and Noble, and other worthy 'High Street' book stores. If you enjoy reading my books half as much as I have enjoyed researching them, then I know you will love them!

Mark Anthony Wyatt

Carbis Bay,
St Ives,
Cornwall
October, 2019.

Cornwall: A Place Apart

Chapter One

This far western end of the south-western British peninsular is a very distinctive, separate place. In past centuries it has had a few different names, including West Waleas, Cernieu, and Cornubia, but is now known as Cornwall, or Kernow. Over 4000 years ago, parts of Britain, including Cornwall, were inhabited by a race of people who had migrated up from the shores of the near east, from areas we now know as Israel, Syria and Palestine. The Celts would arrive later, ousted by the incoming Saxon tribes from more easterly parts of what we now call England. I don't wish to get too bogged down here, or controversial, by going too deep in to the politics and history of Cornwall, it's not the place for it, but it is important to know that the British Island that we now know as comprised of three separate countries: Scotland, Wales, and England, was at one time divided in to four distinct countries: Scotia, Wallia, Anglia, and Cornubia (Cornwall). The border between Devon (an English county) and Cornwall, mostly follows the River Tamar, which flows 61 miles from north to south, and it was agreed upon back in the tenth century, as the dividing line between Anglo-Saxon Wessex, and Celtic Cornwall. The Saxons had by then taken control as far west as Exeter, under the ethnic cleanser, Athelstan, who had savagely murdered, and expelled westwards, the Romano-Cornish-British from the town in 927 AD. However, after that, the Saxons had largely left the Cornish to run their own affairs, beyond the River Tamar to the west, but it is thought that the King of the Cornish, Hywel, had to pay 'tribute' to the Saxons to maintain his autonomy.

The history since those days would require several more books just to scratch the surface, but it is not so relevant here. The Cornish sense of independent national identity has not diminished over the centuries since, indeed, in recent years there has been a resurgence, as Cornish people, including descendants of those who left in the great Cornish diaspora of the 18th and 19th centuries, have increasingly embraced their ancient culture, history, heritage, and even their ancient language. The prolific, talented author, Denys Val Baker, a man born in England of Welsh parents, who adored Cornwall, and lived here for many years before his death in 1984, had this to say:

"Cornwall simply cannot be treated as just another English county. It has always been and will surely remain a place apart, a strange kind of timeless land, in which past, present and future, are all weirdly combined in a welter of images and experiences."

If you are still unsure of where you can find Cornwall on a map of the British Isles, look down to the south-west of England and you will see Cornwall, it's the end part of the peninsular, sticking out 90 miles westwards from the River Tamar, slightly resembling a crooked finger pointing out in to the Atlantic Ocean. Cornwall is no more than 40 miles wide, south to north, at any given point, and progressively, from east to west, it is less. To the north of the extreme west of Cornwall, across the Celtic Sea, lies the far south west of Wales, the south coast of Ireland, and the Irish Sea. To the south of Cornwall, across the English Channel, lies Brittany in the west of France, a region of close Celtic kinship. To the east of Cornwall, the River Tamar, if it had continued just over three and a half miles further northwards, up towards the Bristol Channel, would have formed a complete natural border with the county of Devon, in England. Cornwall then, you could say, is very nearly an island.

The geography, geology, cultural heritage, and history of this ancient land, not only reinforces its natural independence from its eastern neighbour, England, but also influences the spirit of its inhabitants, whether descendants of long established Cornish natives, or more recent immigrants from elsewhere in Britain and the wider world. The bedrock of Cornwall, of which a very high proportion is granite, may also have something to do with that innate Cornish sense of difference from their English neighbours. The Cornish will always maintain that independent spirit, it may say 'England' on our modern maps, but we all know that once we cross the River Tamar, travelling east to west, crossing over I.K. Brunel's wonderful bridge, we are no longer really in England.

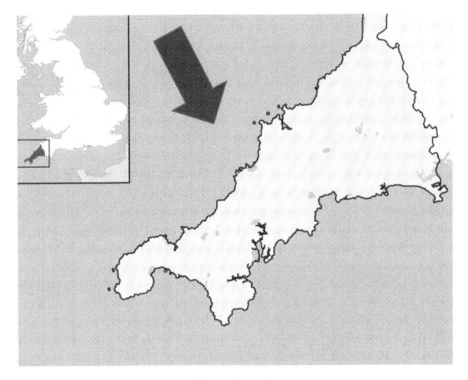

We are Here!

UFOs over the Milky Way

Chapter Two

I feel that this joint UFO witness account, by a father and daughter, is as good a place as any to begin my book, as their UFOs were sighted over the isolated, rural, Cornish/Devon border. However, I doubt that our visitors would have seen any distinction between being over Cornwall or Devon from their altitude; to a visitor up there, from 'out there' (or perhaps another dimension, time-line, or even living here alongside us) the green fields, hedgerows, trees, farms, country roads, cottages, village churches, miles and miles of winding coast-line, and river estuaries, probably all look much the same!

I first met Derek Thomas on-line, when I was living in Bude, on the North Cornish coast, around 12 years ago, via his involvement with David Gillham's Truro-based Cornwall UFO Research Group. Although I wasn't aware of it at first, Derek only lived about half a mile away from my home. We had been talking one day about ghosts, and during that conversation, when Derek mentioned some Bude area hauntings, the penny had suddenly dropped that we were practically neighbours. We soon arranged to meet up for a coffee and a proper chin-wag, and to this day we still get together every now and then to catch-up. Derek is originally from the Black Country, in the Midlands of England. He settled in Bude around 30 years ago. He is a youthful looking retiree, a father of three, and a grandfather to six. He keeps himself very active, mostly by helping others less fortunate than himself, which is admirable in itself since he has had to cope with more than his fair share of serious personal health issues. A few years ago he set up a 'drop-in, meet-up' local group, for isolated people who needed to have a more sociable life. They all set out as total strangers to each other, but now, thanks to Derek, they are all old friends. That's the kind of guy he is, a better friend would be hard to find.

Derek's UFO sighting took place on a bright, clear, sunny afternoon, not that far from the Cornwall/Devon border, in 1995, when he was not quite 50 years old. He had occasionally experienced paranormal activity since he was a young lad, but had not, up until that day, taken that much interest in the UFO subject. This experience that I'm about to relate opened him up to paying more attention to the subject, and doing lots more research in to the supernatural. Derek was in his car with his daughter Debbie, who was just 21 at the time, driving north-eastwards from Bude, up the meandering Atlantic Highway (the A39), close to the 'Atlantic Village' shopping and leisure complex, and the 'Milky Way' (hence the chapter title) holiday theme park, to pick up his son. As they were driving along, doing around 50/60 mph, Debbie had noticed a strange looking anomaly up in the sky, "What's that up there dad?" She had said. Derek leaned over towards her front passenger seat on his left to take a quick peek at where she was pointing. "Oh, that, it's probably just a plane of some sort," he had replied. Derek couldn't, at that stage, he told me, get a really good look at it, and he admitted his response had been a bit hasty. In any case, Debbie hadn't been at all convinced by her dad's answer. Continuing to stare upwards at the strange unknown aerial craft, she confidently said, "Dad, I don't think it is."

For the next few minutes they both tried to keep their eyes on the odd craft, which was much harder for Derek of course as he was driving. Derek observed that it clearly wasn't a conventional plane. He later told me, "It stood out plainly on a very blue, cloudless sky," going on to add, "it was like a brilliant white horizontal tube."

Derek was alternating between watching the road ahead of him and watching the strange object up in the sky. When he looked up again, he had noted, to his amazement, that the horizontal tube appeared to be now standing on its end! Derek was struggling to keep his eyes on the tube for too long, only able to grab swift glimpses, as he was obviously trying to drive safely too, but Debbie, without that responsibility, was far freer to follow its progress more comprehensively.

As they approached a large traffic roundabout island, Derek had slowed right down, to around 10/15 mph, in order to take a longer look at the weird tubular craft. He drove through the roundabout far slower than he would normally have done, like an elderly Sunday driver on an afternoon drive in the country. Derek unwound his side window, then peered up intently at the UFO, now directly over him, he could clearly make out odd markings on the underside of the odd craft. On the other side of the roundabout there was a big lay-by on his left. Derek says that ever since that day, he has often puzzled over why he never thought to pull over in to it, so he could have got out of the car, and taken a better look at the strange aerial craft. It would have been so easy for him to do so, he had even got a good quality pair of binoculars in his car's glove box.

This is something that is often reported when people see a UFO, it's as if the excitement of the incident temporarily interferes with their normal thought processes and reactions, or are they perhaps being influenced by some unknown intelligence to not take photos or film footage? I have had similar experiences myself, where I have seen something really odd, but somehow, inexplicably, I have failed to do the obvious, get my camera out, and would later admonish myself.

The last Derek and Debbie saw of the UFO that day was when it dropped down behind the tree-line. Derek told me, "We went down the hill, and, once we got to the bottom of the hill, we both watched it go down behind the trees, but we didn't speak much to each other at that point about the strange sighting. I continued to drive on, until we'd reached the traffic island, the one just before Bideford Bridge. I then asked Debbie to have a look around to see if she could still see the UFO. Debbie slipped her safety belt off, then twisted around to have a thorough look behind the car, and all around; but she couldn't see it anymore." It was then that Derek asked, "What did you see Debbie?" She said, "Well, at first, I saw a vertical tube shape, but that then turned in to a triangular shape, just before it went briefly behind the trees. After it re-emerged from the trees, I saw three balls, two at the top, and one at the bottom, it looked like an old pawnbroker's sign, but you could actually see clear blue sky between each of them, they were like separate balls." Derek told Debbie that he had initially seen a brilliant white horizontal tube, which had then transformed in to a brilliant white vertical tube, and had then finally morphed in to squares with rounded corners. It is very common for two witnesses to the same paranormal event to see the same event in a different way, it crops up on witness reports time and again.

Derek and Debbie received some collaborating evidence after their joint UFO sighting. In the spring of 1996, Derek had contacted a man called Bob Boyd. Bob was the top man at the Plymouth UFO Group. Plymouth is a fairly big city, by UK standards, it's situated just across the Tamar River on the Devon side of the Cornish/Devon border, around 60 miles south of where Derek and Debbie had their UFO sighting. Derek had first become aware of Bob whilst searching for information on UFOs, the day after their joint sighting, in a very limited collection of UFO related books at Bude Library. In one of those books, right at the rear, he had seen Bob's contact details, which he had immediately written down, making the call to Bob later that same night; he was keen to get some answers and closure after their sighting.

Bob was very interested in their joint UFO sighting, he asked them to independently fill out a witness testimony form, to give comprehensive details, and to make drawings of what they had seen. They quickly did so, in separate rooms, then sent the information back to Bob. Bob got in touch with Derek soon afterwards, and he told him some welcome news. Apparently, a couple in Dorset, a county east of Devon, had described seeing a UFO that very closely resembled the descriptions that both he and Debbie had supplied in their witness reports.

That is the benefit of reporting UFO sightings to an official body, whether it's the huge American based MUFON organisation, or a more local UFO research group. It helps serious researchers track sightings across country, gives credence and support to witnesses, and helps serious UFO researchers get a better understanding of UFO activity generally. Thanks to the professionalism of Bob Boyd linking those reports together, we now have a credible, measureable, sequence of events, tracking the weird UFO across the West Country of England.

A few days after their joint sighting, whilst driving, Derek had been listening to an interesting conversation about UFOs on BBC Radio Cornwall. The host of the show, Laurence Reed, had struck Derek as mature and professional in his approach to the subject, as did the knowledgeable guest; there were no childish, ill-informed jibes about 'little green men' or 'anal probes,' just plenty of sensible questions and observations. The guest that Laurence was interviewing that day was David Gillham, the founder (in that same year) of the Truro based Cornwall UFO Research Group, a wonderful man who had, quite late in life, become a 'truth-seeker,' especially in regard to the subject of UFOs. I will be mentioning David Gillham occasionally throughout this first volume, and also in volume two, where there will be a tribute to him. He is, in my opinion, one of the two most influential people in the Cornish paranormal world, the other being Michael Williams, and I'll be discussing

Michael's incredible supernatural legacy later too. It speaks so highly of their calibre, that I consider them to be even more influential than more famous paranormal writers/researchers with Cornish connections, who themselves made huge contributions to the Cornish paranormal world, gifted people such as Colin Wilson and Peter Underwood.

At the end of the BBC Radio Cornwall conversation between David Gillham and Laurence Reed, David had given out his telephone number, and website details, to the listening Cornish public. Derek quickly pulled off the road, in order to write David's phone number down on the back of an old fag packet, the only bit of paper he could find! He rang David that same night, and they had a long, interesting, mutually beneficial conversation. The best part of that conversation for Derek was the information that David had only just received that day, from two lads down in the far west of Cornwall, on the south coast at Newlyn, near Penzance. Newlyn is around 100 miles south west of where Derek and Debbie saw their UFO. David excitedly told Derek that the two lads had seen a strange craft in the sky over Newlyn, and that their reported timing fitted in perfectly with what Derek and Debbie saw up by the Cornish border near 'the Milky Way.' The lads had also sent David a good, clear photo of the strange aerial craft, which can still be seen on the Cornwall UFO Research Group's website. Their descriptions, written down on the CUFO Research Group's witness testimony forms, had very closely matched the independent descriptions, and drawings, given to David in Truro, and Bob in Plymouth, by Derek and Debbie. It seems to me that it's highly likely that they all saw the same UFO and, between them, they helped to track the craft from Newlyn in West Cornwall to Dorset, via the Cornwall/Devon border.

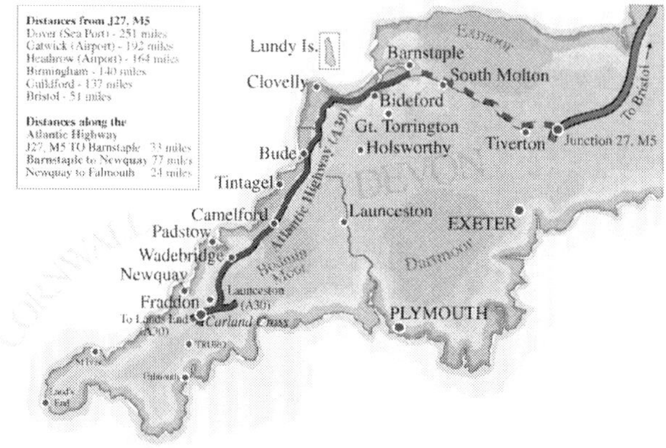

Distances from J27, M5
Dover (Sea Port) - 251 miles
Gatwick (Airport) - 192 miles
Heathrow (Airport) - 164 miles
Birmingham - 140 miles
Guildford - 137 miles
Bristol - 51 miles
Distances along the Atlantic Highway
J27, M5 TO Barnstaple 33 miles
Barnstaple to Newquay 77 miles
Newquay to Falmouth 24 miles
Lundy Is.
Barnstaple
South Molton
Clovelly
Bideford
Gt. Torrington
Holsworthy
Tiverton
Junction 27, M5
To Bristol
Exmoor
Bude
Tintagel
Atlantic Highway (A39)
DEVON
Camelford
Padstow
Wadebridge
Newquay
Fraddon
Launceston
EXETER
Dartmoor
Bodmin Moor
Launceston (A30)
Carland Cross
PLYMOUTH

The A39 Atlantic Highway. Derek and Debbie's UFO sighting took place a few miles north of Bude, near the border with Devon.

A Buddy Song

Chapter Three

Danny was only 64 when he died from cancer. In life, Danny was a skilled builder who had mostly worked on his own, he'd been a fairly frequent visitor to Travis Perkins Builders Merchants, at around the time of the new Millennium, when I was working there as a heating and plumbing materials buyer, after having moved to Bude in the summer of 1999. Danny was one of those blokes you either loved or hated, a bit like Marmite I suppose, or Tina Turner; but I loved the guy from day one. We had many happy times together, putting the world to rights, bantering, laughing and just playing our guitars.

Danny, a divorced father of two young adult girls, was a fairly typical South Londoner of his generation, loud, brash, and not in the least bit politically correct, he was the salt of the earth, one of the best men I ever knew; and I still miss his company. Danny was what older generations used to call a rough diamond; a tough bloke with a heart of gold. Let's just say that I can't tell some of his more youthful stories here. Danny was around six feet tall, lean, and muscular, with hands the size of shovels. He had that mean, street fighter look about him, definitely not somebody you would have messed with; Danny was as hard as nails. In his younger days he had been a member of a tough South London street gang, and when I say tough, I mean tough with a capital 'T,' not like some of those soft (alleged) gangsters today, the ludicrous podgy ones who stumble around exposing their underpants, their trousers somehow miraculously suspended just below their bum cheeks. They wouldn't have survived in post-war South London, but, on the other hand, Danny and his mates may have died laughing.

Despite his obvious toughness, Danny was a sensitive, caring man too, he loved his family and friends, and treated everybody with respect and decency. He was a creative, skilled man, a natural builder, great fun to be around, and a good musician. Danny taught me basic guitar, the simple three chord stuff, and almost every song that he ever tried to teach me was what he would call a 'Buddy song,' he adored Buddy Holly, Johnny Cash and Marty Wilde, and 1950s Rock and Roll generally.

Danny visited the U.S. a few times, he loved it over there. On his last trip, in the 1970s, he had been working his way around the country on a long visa, taking in such geographically diverse places as Texas, New York State and California. To cut a long story short, Danny's visa expired and he couldn't get it extended. Since Danny was having the time of his life, he hadn't wanted to go home, and so he decided he would stay in America anyway! That was the kind of bloke he was, impulsive, not one to care too much about rules and regulations, it was to be the beginning of a comical cat and mouse chase across America, with lots of very close calls. Danny continued to work anywhere that he could, travel, play his guitar, meet new girls, and make even more friends.

Employers in the States loved Danny, as he was a hard worker, bright, amiable and amusing. With help from his workmates and employers, Danny was always one step ahead of the immigration teams tasked with catching him, hoping to send him back to dear ol' Blighty. Many of Danny's temporary bosses turned a blind eye to him not having official permission to stay in the country, and more than a few of them lied to immigration officials who landed at their businesses, saying, when presented with Danny's image, that they'd, "Never seen the guy before," but would, "keep an eye out," for him. Danny, of course, would usually only be a few feet away from the immigration officials, hiding, and stifling his giggles, in a broom cupboard, or perhaps a rest room. Eventually, of course, the immigration guys did catch up with Danny. They (the government) even paid for his flight back home to London, but they had insisted on staying on the plane, either side of Danny, until just before take-off, to ensure that he was still on the plane when it took-off and left for the U.K.!

Danny's funeral signalled for me the beginning of an exodus of my loved ones, not that I knew it then, but my dad, mum, my mates Maurice and Mark, and a few others, would all follow Danny in the years to come. At the funeral, whilst standing over his open grave, Danny's youngest daughter, Emily, a talented musician too, played a 'Buddy song,' perhaps the greatest one of them all, the beautiful, tender 'True Love Ways.' I watched as Emily's tears dripped down the acoustic guitar's neck, making it harder still for her to play on such a sad day. It was one of the most touching moments I have ever experienced at a funeral, I don't mind admitting that I welled up.

When Danny was still around, he often played his 'Buddy songs' very loud in his car, as he was moving around the small town going about his everyday business. It was not uncommon for me, and other people who knew Danny, to hear the distant sounds of 'Peggy Sue Got Married,' or perhaps 'Rave On,' and then have him honk his horn at us, as he drove by, smiling and waving a few minutes later.

A month or so after Danny had passed, Sally, Danny's eldest daughter, was hard at work at her office, on a warm summer morning in Bude. The first-floor office window was wide open, letting a light breeze in; it over-looked the single carriage road by Bude Golf Club's club-house, and the lush green golf links rolling over towards Flexbury. Suddenly, Sally had heard the sound of a car approaching with very loud music blaring out. It had slowly become more distinct, she recognised it as a Buddy Holly song, 'Everyday.' Sally instinctively jumped out of her seat, almost spilling her coffee as she did so, and, without really thinking it through, she had rushed over towards the open window to see her dad driving by, something that she had done dozens of times before. The Buddy song got closer and closer, before it finally passed right by her office. But sadly for Sally, there were no cars passing by, and no happy, smiling dad, waving that huge hand out of the car window. Sally shivered, her eyes welled up. It had dawned on her that her dad was gone. But she could still faintly hear the Buddy song, as it moved away in to the distance, and she knew that her dad's love for her, and her sister Emily, would 'not fade away.'

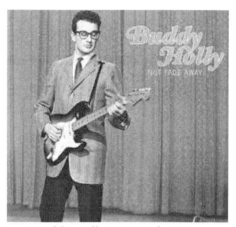

Buddy Holly, Not Fade Away

The Grenville Ghost
(a simple twist of fate)
Chapter Four

Simon, better known to his many friends as Skatman, lived and surfed in and around Bude on the North Cornish coast. A happy go lucky Cornish lad, an optimist who enjoyed the opportunities that life sent his way, Skatman's catchphrase was, "Never say never, always say maybe!" Sadly though, for all who knew and loved him, he was tragically taken by a terminal disease in 2012. At the age of only 45 Skatman had caught his last wave here in this world. A few months before his death, Skatman had travelled with his best friend, 'Big Wave Dave,' on what everybody feared would be his last surfing trip overseas. Prior to their trip, Big Wave Dave had asked Skatman what his wishes were if he should die whilst they were away; Skatman's response betrayed his robust character, and the typical Cornish surfers' love of the sea and nature, "Oh, just put me on my board mate and push me out to sea."

In the early summer of 2017, I was on the look-out for a small economical flat, due to my not so bright idea of renting out my St Ives property to tourists, as it was more successful than I had anticipated, leaving me sporadically homeless! I put the word out and pretty soon my friends Jennie and Rob Wilson messaged me to come up to see them; they had a suggestion to make. Rob is an old friend of mine; we first met at around the time of the new Millennium, on the touch-line at Bude Rugby Club on a cold Sunday morning, whilst watching our young lads play, bravely battling it out against the visitors from Bodmin, and I mean battle, one of their ten year-old 'boys' was already fast becoming a Cornish Giant!

Rob and Jennie's boys, Niall, Joe and Luke, are now all young adults, their ages ranging from mid to late twenties. The Wilson's back door is always open to welcome old and new friends alike; the kettle's always on. Their home is like a time-slip back to the 1960s Tillingbourne Valley I grew up in, where the neighbours were always in and out of each other's homes, using the excuse of having run out of sugar, or perhaps coffee, but really just wanting to have a good old chin-wag and cadge a fag. The Wilson's abode is a place where you can find laughter, and, if it's needed, sympathy or advice. I quickly popped up there, keen to hear their suggestion.

Jenny put my coffee on the dining table in front of me, and Rob, who had briefly disappeared in to the sitting room when he'd seen me arriving, had soon returned, smiling, with his old acoustic. He handed the guitar over to me, as he knows I love to pick it when I pop by, but then, just as quickly, he'd grabbed it back again, he just couldn't resist playing his party-piece first, the opening lines of 'Simple Twist of Fate' by Bob Dylan, with exaggerated Dylanisms. I joined in of course, and we laughed as if we'd never ever done it before:

'They sat together in the paaaaaaaarrrkkkkk,

As the evening sky grew daaaaaaaarrrkkkkk.'

Jenny tried not to show that she enjoyed our silliness, she rolled her eyes, then, looking more serious, she'd told me they'd heard from Niall that there was a spare room going down at 'Grenville,' the shared house where he now lived, a large 1970s detached, better known to some Bude folk as 'The Goat House,' due to its historic association with wild parties!

Grenville originally got its name from the centuries old local Grenville family, one of whom was Sir Richard Grenville, the sea Captain of the 'Revenge,' another, Sir Bevil Grenville, was a Royalist Colonel who had fought alongside Sir Ralph Hopton, and the Cornish Giant from Stratton,

Antony Payne, at the Battle of Stamford Hill (mentioned later in this book) in 1643. Grenville was for many years a property owned by local surfing and adventure businesses, used as a multi-occupancy home for surf life-guards, and outdoor adventure instructor employees.

Many of those who have passed through Grenville as residents, over the last 20 to 30 years, return every now and then to check the old place out and to catch up with old friends. It's my belief, and that of many witnesses, that at least one of those ex-tenants, our friend Skatman, still visits Grenville from time to time, but more on that a little later. I was keen to check Grenville out so I hurriedly finished my coffee, got back in the car, and drove down there; a ten minute trip.

The house is situated down the end of a long, winding, rural lane, behind the Crooklets area of Bude, and alongside higher cliff-top fields. Niall welcomed me in the traditional Cornish manner at the door, "Wasson?" Jennie had tipped him off I was on my way, and why. Niall showed me various spare rooms that were available to rent, all overflowing with huge amps, damaged surfboards, dirty rugby shirts, and other assorted paraphernalia, so it was difficult at first to envisage how big the rooms actually were.

We were on the first floor, on our way to look at another vacant room, when I noticed a room by the stairs with a partially opened door. That door offered me tantalising glimpses of distant Bude roof-tops, and the beautiful north coast, heading south-westwards down towards the Camel Estuary at Padstow. I gave Niall a look that must have said I was interested. "Yeah, alright, go on then, but I'm not clearing it out for you mate, you can do that yourself." He smiled and walked away towards his room at the other end of the house, to finish watching a rugby match on the TV that my visit had rudely interrupted.

I carefully made my way in to the room, treading gingerly as I did so, over a surfboard with a big chunk missing, as if it had been nibbled on by a hungry shark off Crooklets Beach. It was obvious that the room had once been the home of a surfer, the driftwood, beach pebbles, fishing floats, and other assorted sea debris stuck on the ceiling, and strewn about the floor, walls, and shelving, were the clues. I called out to Niall, "Who was living here last?" "No idea mate, it hasn't been lived in for at least five years," he had responded.

I hadn't at the time, even considered that he may have been, in a kind way, not telling me everything. There was always a high turnover of tenants at Grenville, it's the sort of place where people only stay for a while, then move on to other gaffes, as and when funds and circumstances allow. The reason for Niall's reticence to tell me too much about the room, would, in the weeks ahead, slowly become more apparent. In the days that followed, I cleaned up and decorated the room in a blue and yellow seaside colour scheme. I was now the proud tenant of a man-shed/office/bedsit, which would soon have most of the things that I needed to be comfortable, including every writer's best friends, a kettle, a mug, a jar of coffee, and a mini-fridge.

Grenville had a happy energy, we enjoyed a shared sense of community, mutual-aid, friendship, and a lot of laughs, especially when our friend Freddie was in residence. He is one of those blokes who always lifts your day. The younger crowd at Grenville soon accepted me as just another friend, despite me being at least thirty years their senior; I mostly enjoyed their company. Maybe it saved me from going the same way as some of my peers, the moaners and groaners; old before their time, those who are always complaining about young people, forgetting that they were all young once too, and older people had moaned about their lifestyles.

Shortly after first moving in, I had begun to hear stories about a guy called Skatman, who, I was beginning to learn, had once been a resident of Grenville. Most of the current tenants had known him, and when speaking of him they always spoke in hushed, respectful terms, as if, even though they were only ever saying pleasant things about him, he might overhear. I thought their reverence a bit odd, assuming at the time that Skatman had merely moved on elsewhere, and was probably living the surfers' dream in Hawaii, Mexico, or perhaps Sri Lanka. But that all began to change when Verity, Freddie's prettier other half, relayed her nocturnal encounters with Skatman's ghost; and that's when the penny had suddenly dropped, Skatman was not overseas as I had assumed, he had obviously died. Noticing my surprise, Verity said, "So, nobody's told you that Skatman actually died here at Grenville, and that he still visits us from time to time?" I cheekily replied, "No, I think I would have remembered that." Verity smiled, "He usually turns up when the house is quiet, or when any of us are at home alone." She went on to say that when she'd seen Skatman, he had been dressed the same way as in life, with his surfing board shorts, and his hair big and wild. Bryony, another lovely young lady who lived at Grenville at the time, had overheard our conversation, and added that she had experienced Skatman's ghost too, and her boyfriend Joe, another ex-tenant, had seen a brief glimpse of Skatman cycling up Maer Lane towards Grenville. I was intrigued by all these sightings, and, if I'm honest, a little bit pleased too, as I love a good ghost story. But this one was a little different, I will admit to having been a little apprehensive at the prospect of meeting Skatman in the early hours of the morning.

Bryony said that Joe had been coming home in his big work van, up dark, twisting Maer Lane, to Grenville, in the early hours of the morning, when he'd suddenly seen, in his headlights, somebody on a bike ahead of him, just by the old entrance to the Bude Holiday Park. Taking care to not knock that person off their bike, Joe had slowed right down as he approached cautiously from behind, giving the cyclist time to be aware of his presence. Joe carefully drove around the cyclist in the very narrow, pot-holed lane, and, as he passed, he looked to his right to see if he knew the cyclist. To his surprise, Joe had immediately recognised the man on the bike as his deceased friend Skatman! By now, a few feet in front of the cyclist, Joe, obviously shocked and confused, checked his right wing mirror to look at the cyclist again; Skatman and his bike were no longer there. There is no way any cyclist could have disappeared that quickly, as there were no exit points off the narrow lane.

More ghostly revelations soon followed, as I began to settle in to my space at Grenville. Stell is your typical Cornish surfer, laid-back, bright and articulate. He had called by Grenville to catch up with any old mates who might be around. Having not met before we had introduced ourselves at the foot of the stairs, just below my room. He told me a little bit about himself, his work as a life-guard, and the happy days he'd spent living at Grenville. "Which room are you living in Mark?" He asked me quietly, I gestured with my forefinger upstairs to my room. There was a short pause as his gaze followed my finger's response, he looked back at me, "You DO know Skatman rented that room don't you?" 'I do now,' I replied. Until that moment, I hadn't really known for sure that Skatman had been the previous tenant, but had begun to suspect it due to occasional feelings of a benign presence in my room. We chatted some more about Skatman, and my new house-mate's sightings. He then hinted that he had experienced something strange himself. I told him I was a writer, that I was putting a book together about peoples' paranormal experiences in Cornwall, and said I'd love to hear his story, if he ever wanted to share it. Stell generously agreed to share his experience. Apparently, he'd been walking back up Maer Lane from the Crooklets area of Bude, after meeting some mates in the town. It was around 1:00 am, not that long after Skatman had passed, and he was walking by the old entrance to Bude

Holiday Park, where Joe had his sighting. Stell had clearly heard the sound of a cyclist coming up very fast behind him, and had instinctively thrown himself, back first, against the brambles and hawthorns, on the steep-sided Cornish hedge bank to his right, so as to quickly get out of the way of the on-coming cyclist. As he landed roughly against the hedge, Stell looked back towards where he thought the cyclist would be, but there was no cyclist. He said the experience had given him the chills, an energy had passed right through him, and, as it did so, he had instantly visualised his old mate Skatman; he was laughing.

Everybody who lived alongside me at Grenville seemed to be sensitive to some degree, whether or not they knew it. One fellow tenant said he often heard Skatman walking around the house when everybody else was out during the day, and occasionally in the early hours of the morning too. I was sat in my room discussing the Skatman presence with an American friend in the early hours of the morning, and weirdly, just after I had mentioned Skatman's name, there had been a HUGE impact on Grenville's exterior wall. It had felt like a wave of energy hitting the house, which had then momentarily shook. I was shocked, not knowing what to make of it. I told my friend on the phone what I had just experienced, and she said, "Did anybody else hear it?" I told her I'd let her know in a few minutes, as I was already on the way downstairs to find out. I went in to the sitting-room, which was directly under my room. My son Dexter was in there with his mate Mezz, quietly playing together on the Play-Station. "Did you just feel that massive bang that shook the walls?" I asked. I instantly had their attention, they both looked up and responded immediately, and in unison:

"Yeah! What the **** was it?" I smiled.

"I have absolutely no idea, I was hoping that you would know!"

Another witness to Skatman's presence around Bude, since his untimely passing in 2012, was Alex, much better known to his many friends as

'Buttercup,' the head chef of David Sibley's excellent Life's a Beach café, down on Summerleaze Beach in Bude, where Skatman once worked. I know Buttercup's family quite well, his dad, Mark, is a Bude postman, and a good friend, we first met whilst working together at the Royal Mail in Bude. For a few years, I also cut the grass, and pruned the apple trees for his lovely wife, Loraine, at their beautiful country cottage at Marhamchurch, on the outskirts of Bude. Our connections don't end there, my kids were at school with theirs; Ryan, James and Alex are a bright, fun, friendly bunch of lads. Anyway, here's Buttercup to tell you about his strange experiences at the café:

"I have had two major strange experiences since I began working at the Life's a Beach café several years ago, and I remember them both very clearly. The first of these was not that long after Skatman had died. I know for sure that I was on my own in the café, everybody else having already left for the night, I was locking up. I suddenly caught, out of the corner of my eye, something moving. It quickly became more distinct; it was somebody headed for the rear door. It all happened so fast, but I recognised that somebody almost immediately-- it was Skatman! (Skatman used to work at the café.) It was his hair that was the major clue, Skat always had this really big crazy strawberry blonde hair, kind of ruffled, and really distinctive, he was known for it. I knew that the rear door had previously been closed, and yet, somehow, when I saw Skatman approaching it, and passing through it, it had been half-opened. As I said, I know there was nobody else around in the café at that time, it gave me a bit of a shock, and it's still difficult for me to wrap my head around what I experienced that night all these years later, as I'm telling you about it now. I'm not a firm believer in ghosts to be honest, and yet I know what I saw that night: Skatman leaving the café.

My second strange experience at the café was also connected to Skat. At the time, I was living above the café, I had my own on-suite room up there. I was hanging out in my room late one night, after having done a late shift cheffing in the café. I was with my mate Mark, who was also working there at the time. We had decided to go back downstairs, in to the now deserted café, to grab ourselves a couple of cold ones (beers) from the fridge, and we then sat ourselves down to look out the big windows at the beach, sea and stars, and have a chat. Mark had not long returned from some spiritual, hippy type retreat in Ibiza, and he was telling me about what he had experienced and learnt there. I confided in Mark, about my sighting of Skat leaving the building by the back door, and we'd somehow then got around to talking about séances and communicating with the dead, that sort of thing. We had both been good friends of Skat, and, inevitably I suppose, that conversation had led us in to trying to contact him. I asked out loud if Skat was present in the café, not really expecting any response, but we both got a bit of a shock as the bank cash/card machine had suddenly made a loud beeping noise, immediately after my question had been asked, as if in response, and then, even weirder than that, the payment screen had come on too! To get that to show up on the machine you had to physically press a button, we were the only people in the café, and we were nowhere near close enough to have touched any buttons on that machine, that really gave me the 'willies' pretty good I can tell you!"

I met Buttercup's friend, ex-workmate, and fellow witness, Mark, shortly after receiving Buttercup's witness testimony, and he had confirmed everything that Buttercup had told me. We were chatting at the foot of the stairs at Grenville. At one point of our brief conversation, Mark had pointed up to my room and said, "You DO know that your room is the room where Skatman died don't you?" I let that information slowly sink in, then responded, "Yes, I do now Mark." Before adding, "Stell told me that Skatman lived in my room, but I didn't know, until you just told me, that he had actually died in there. Thanks for telling me that." It was meant as sarcasm, but I remember shivering.

During the research I did to find out more about Skatman for this chapter, I was advised by Niall to check-out a couple of video tributes to him, on-line at YouTube. In one, a smiling Skatman talks to a BBC camera crew, telling them:

"Surfing is the best sport in the world!"

There's also touching footage of the paddle out in his honour, and the scattering of his ashes in to the bay, over-looked by the café, that he loved to surf. After first viewing the video footage of Skatman, it occurred to me that I had met him too, shortly after I first moved in to Grenville. His image was so familiar, the strawberry blonde hair, the beaming smile, the board shorts, and that cap. It had dawned on me that he was the surfer dude that I had very briefly glimpsed in Grenville's kitchen.

At around 10:00 am, I was doing some washing up at the sink, still half asleep, my brain in neutral; idly looking out of the rear window at a couple of squirrels playing on the garden wall behind one of the campers in the holiday park. A bloke had suddenly, and quite unexpectedly, appeared behind me, a few feet away to my left, by the entrance door. I heard a man's voice say something, I think it was, "Wasson" and I had turned around to see who had said it. It was a busy place, people were always coming and going, and I didn't yet know all of them. I had responded, "Hi," then just looked back towards the soapy dishes in the sink. I didn't pay him that much attention really, and I assumed that after he passed by behind me, he would have just gone up the stairs to see Niall, who as far as I knew, was in his room, asleep, or watching the TV. I had just assumed he must have been a tenant that I hadn't yet been introduced to, or perhaps a friend of one of the tenants. I never saw that surfer dude again at Grenville, or anywhere else around Bude, and it is a very small community.

While I was in the USA in the spring of 2018, I heard, via my son Dexter's e-mail, the shocking news that an eviction notice had been served, by Cornwall Council (local government) on all of the tenants at Grenville. They had decided that the owner of the property hadn't complied with certain rules governing multiple-tenancies. This sad news put everybody in a bit of a spin, but fortunately, with zero credit to Cornwall Council, who clearly didn't care that they had put several young Bude people at serious risk of homelessness, all of Grenville's young tenants did manage to find alternative accommodation.

I hurried back from Illinois to remove my belongings from Grenville. As I was helping Dexter to clear out two large attic spaces, and a garage full of many years' worth of accumulated items, including multiple surfboards, body boards, wetsuits, mountain-boards, outdoor sports clothing, and other adventure sports equipment, we found some of Skatman's private possessions in some dusty boxes buried under assorted junk. These included a few photos of Skatman with his old mates, ex-Grenville tenants and visitors. Some of the photos were hilarious; there had clearly been a harmless, fun, initiation game, that earlier Grenville tenants had enjoyed inflicting on new house mates and friends who called by. Their victim would have to pose naked behind a surfboard for a photograph, and that photo was then subsequently stuck on to the big fridge for all to see! They were a young, glamorous, athletic, attractive group, I'm pleased the practice had ceased by the time I arrived at Grenville!

I took all the photos, and Skatman's other personal bits and pieces, up to his brother Max, who, I had recently been told by Niall, owned a motorbike business in Bude. I had never met Max before, and to say I was apprehensive would be an understatement. Max wasn't expecting to meet me, so for him to suddenly, out of the blue, be confronted, not only with some of his deceased brother's personal effects, but also a request from a complete stranger to write his brother's ghost story, must have been very hard for him. (Sorry Max!) I was trying to be tactful and respectful in a difficult situation; but, despite my best efforts, it was unavoidably emotional. Sensing Max's discomfort, I had taken my cue, and, leaving his brother's personal items with him, I had asked him to think it all over, and then get in touch with me, if and when he was ready. I needn't have worried so much, Max was very understanding, and open-minded. A few weeks later I got a pleasant message from Max, he said he'd thought it all over, had talked to family and friends, and was giving me his blessing to go ahead, provided I fixed a few minor inaccuracies, which I did.

Many ex-tenants, and other friends of Grenville, dropped by to say goodbye to the old house, as word quickly travelled around Bude of the final, sad demise of Grenville, and of course the infamous, Goat House parties too. Many local people were upset to see Grenville dying, and die it will, as the rumours are that a builder will buy Grenville, then knock it down to do a new-build on the site.

You may recall, earlier in this chapter, I had called on my friends Rob and Jennie, with regard to finding a suitable property to rent. It has only now occurred to me, that my visit to see Rob and Jennie that day, had heralded a turn of events in my life that would lead me to writing Skatman's story. I wonder if it was a 'simple twist of fate' that led me to Grenville that day, or was it perhaps Skatman himself who had orchestrated my move there, from beyond the veil, in order for his story to be told to the wider world?

After Skatman died in 2012, his friends in the Bude surfing community arranged a touching tribute to his memory. One Sunday morning a large crowd gathered on the Bude cliff-tops and Summerleaze Beach, to pay their last respects to a Bude legend. Many of Skatman's surfing friends, well over a hundred of them, paddled out on their surfboards, to just beyond Bude's Breakwater, where they all formed a big circle, sitting up on their boards, arms linked. In the middle of that circle, bobbing about, was a small Bude R.N.L.I. (Royal National Lifeboat Institute) orange lifeboat, crewed by local Bude men and women who were Skatman's friends. The lifeboat crew scattered Skatman's ashes in to the bay where he so loved to surf, then there was a minute's silence, as his old friends retreated in to their own private thoughts and memories. This was followed by a rousing round of applause for Skatman by everybody present, and by the traditional Cornish chant:

Oggy Oggy Oggy!

Oi Oi Oi!

Oggy Oggy Oggy!

Oi Oi Oi!

Oggy!

Oi!

Oggy!

Oi!

Oggy Oggy Oggy!

Oi Oi Oi!

Will Skatman's ghost continue to haunt the Life's a Beach Café, Maer Lane, or the Grenville site? As Skatman used to say:

"Never say never, always say maybe!"

But, if you don't find him there, he'll probably be in the line-up with his old Bude buddies who pre-deceased him, and others who have joined him since, surfing off a golden sandy beach in paradise, where the wind is always light off-shore, and the waves glassy, awaiting his turn to shred!

In memory of Simon, aka Skatman, a Bude surfing legend, 1967-2012. He's missed by all those who were lucky enough to have known him. Skatman RIPs!

Haunted Maer Lane, Bude

UFOs over GCHQ

Chapter Five

Twenty two years ago, and not that far from where Skatman loved to surf, my friend Tom Dell was on a ten week woodland survival course, on the wooded cliff-tops and fertile fields near GCHQ, the 'Top Secret' British and American Government facility. There were six people taking part, two course leaders, John and Emily, and four trainees, Jim, Sally, Jane and Tom. On the last night of the course, the plan was to have a social evening around a camp-fire, tell a few stories, get to know each other a little better, and then sleep out together under the stars, in shelters made from natural materials, picked up in the fields and woods all around. It had been a lovely mid-summer's day, Tom and his colleagues had been looking forward to spending the night in such a tranquil, scenic location.

At about 10:00 pm, as the sun had at last begun to set, Tom asked Emily if it would be OK if he climbed up a nearby hill to look out over the cliffs and sea, to watch the sun going down. It was the perfect place to be on such a night. Emily, who was jointly legally responsible, along with John, for the safety of all the trainees, had looked to John for confirmation. John looked at Tom, smiled, then at Emily, and then nodded. Emily, smiling, said, 'Yes, that's fine Tom, but please take a safety whistle with you, just in case you should fall and hurt yourself, you can't be too careful." Tom thanked Emily and John, took the whistle that Emily handed him, hung it around his neck, and then, looking around at the group, asked if anybody else wanted to go up the hill with him, but, surprisingly for Tom, nobody took him up on his offer. So off he had gone on his own.

It was spectacular up there, well worth the climb. Tom sat and watched a little fishing boat coming in to the bay far below him, and from his high vantage point it looked as if the fishing boat was an 'Airfix' model. Gradually, as the minutes ticked by, the sunlight slowly began to fade, the sun sinking slowly in to the sea on the horizon. After a long, hot sunny day, it had become dark and chilly very quickly. Tom noticed the spotlights at the GCHQ facility, they were beginning to turn on, one by one, illuminating the scene. He decided to get his camera from his bag, to take some photos of the huge early warning dishes, as they were now glowing prettily due to those spotlights. The camera he used that night was a Nokia 35, Tom took four shots of the GCHQ base, with approximately nine seconds between each click of his camera. He didn't check the pictures at the time, preferring to wait until he was at home the next morning, when he could see the results on his larger computer screen. Just as Tom finished snapping the fourth photo he had begun to feel inexplicably spooked, uneasy, but had no idea why, then the silence had been abruptly shattered by two RAF military jets (Royal Air Force) roaring right over the GCHQ base. The jets had come up from the south, on a northern heading, quickly heading out over the Bristol Channel in the direction of South Wales. It was then that Tom had noticed an intense bright light behind him, swiftly growing in size, weaving its way through the woods, and headed directly down towards him, Tom had shivered, the hairs on the back of his neck had stood up; he headed back to the safety of numbers.

When Tom finally got back down the hill, slightly out of breath, the odd light had temporarily retreated back in to the woods. The rest of the team were just beginning to stir from the dying embers of the camp-fire, where they had spent the evening telling stories; they were now headed for their make-shift beds. Tom decided to keep his story and unease to himself, thinking that it might upset his colleagues, and that his unease would soon pass, but he just couldn't relax. Tom's nervousness continued, he couldn't figure out why. All night long he tossed and turned in his bed, he just couldn't sleep, he could hear muffled voices and movements in the woods all around, but the other members of the team were sleeping soundly through it. Tom kept seeing glimpses of something quick, shadowy, and dark, he wasn't sure exactly what that something was, but he felt sure it was stalking them.

The next morning, back at home again in Stratton, just a few miles away, weary from lack of sleep, Tom logged on to his computer to upload the photos he had taken the previous night. Tom was only really hoping for a few pretty pictures; but he got far more than he had bargained for! The second of the four photos of the GCHQ base's big dishes really surprised him, it showed a clear dark distinctive shape in the centre of the photo, hovering over the GCHQ top-secret base; and it looked like a tear-drop shaped UFO. When he had snapped the pictures he had definitely not seen a UFO with his naked eyes, or through the view-finder, visibility had been good, and there hadn't been any clouds, just a clear night sky. I have seen all of those photos, and I could clearly make out the tear-drop shaped UFO in the second of the four photos too, you can't really not see it. By using very basic enhancing tools on my laptop, I was able, by changing colours etcetera, to make it even more clear and blatant. The anomaly can be viewed on the Cornwall UFO Research Group web-site, if you request to see it, via either David Gillham, or Derek Thomas.

Tom's neighbour works at the GCHQ camp, he's a computer systems engineer in a fairly senior post, and so, for his protection, I have changed his name here to Bill. He's one of many computer systems experts who live around Bude and are employed at the base. All GCHQ employees have to sign the Official Secrets Act upon taking up their posts, as they deal with sensitive, highly classified information on a daily basis. It is well known around Bude that the base is run by the CIA and NSA. I strongly suspect that some of the GCHQ personnel know far more about our 'visitors' than they are allowed to share with the public.

Tom had often chatted with Bill, they always got on well, and he had always seemed like an open minded man. That morning Bill had been pottering around in his front garden, tinkering with his hydrangeas. Tom was curious to get Bill's opinion on the anomalous image that he had accidentally captured on his camera, and so he went outside to engage Bill in conversation. Tom jumped straight in, abandoning any pretence of small talk, asking Bill outright if he had ever seen a UFO. Bill had looked up from his prized hydrangeas, taken aback by such a sudden, random question, a bemused look on his face, and, for a few seconds, Tom thought that Bill was deciding whether he could confide in him. Bill must have decided that Tom was trustworthy, as he had then proceeded to tell him about a huge black triangle shaped UFO that he, and several other GHCHQ personnel, had seen sitting directly over the GCHQ base a few years earlier, "It completely blocked out the stars Tom, it was huge!" Bill had said. He went on to say that security staff at the base had made an official report of its visit. Tom was now even more intrigued, he beckoned Bill, "Please come with me Bill, just for a few minutes, I think you might be interested in what I have got to show you."

Tom took Bill in to his front room to see the full-screen sized photo on his computer. Bill was very attentive and curious, he looked closely at the image, but hadn't seemed that surprised. Unfazed by Bill's nonchalant attitude, Tom excitedly told Bill about the events of the previous night. Bill listened intently, then said, "The planes that you mentioned Tom, were they two RAF jets?"

"Yes," Tom had responded, "they were," puzzled by the reason that Bill would ask that particular question. "How would you know that Bill?"

"Yes Tom, I thought there would have been, they always send two jets up to engage with the visitors." Tom was surprised that Bill had said it so calmly, so matter-of-factly, as if he were discussing something far more mundane, like how to keep bugs off his lupins.

GCHQ, near Bude

What follows are three more witness testimonies to strange aerial anomalies seen in and around the GCHQ/Bude area in recent years.

Graham's Story

Graham was walking his dog near Crooklets Beach, at Bude, around 7:30 pm one evening, when he saw what at first had looked like a very bright star. Graham said that it was the incredible intense brightness that had initially caught his attention. As he watched it, he noticed that the bright star was moving very slowly, about a mile or so out from the beach; then it had suddenly just stopped dead in its tracks. Graham said that the 'star' (obviously by now he had realized it wasn't a star) never once flashed, as is sometimes reported by UFO witnesses, and that it was totally silent. To his absolute amazement two smaller, yellowish orb lights shot out of the side of the bigger orb light, and they had then sped off together, almost playfully, like dancing children, south westwards down the Cornish coast towards the Tintagel area, some twenty plus miles away. Graham said that they moved so fast that they were down there in a heartbeat. Then the bigger bright orb just went straight up, incredibly fast, and very high, until it had vanished from view, leaving the smaller orbs still somewhere around the Tintagel area. Graham was surprised, later that evening, and the next day, that nobody else was reporting seeing the UFOs, and to this day he remains very confused as to what it actually was that he witnessed that night.

Kim's Story

Kim from Bude was out walking in the early hours of the morning with her dog, on Bude's golf course by the coast. She was in the area close to the rear of the Meadow Drive housing estate, when she had suddenly spotted three huge orbs hovering over the golf greens. "They were kind of cloudy in appearance," she remembered, "and they were clearly under some kind of intelligent control." She watched as they headed back out towards the coast by Summerleaze Beach. Kim said she had felt scared, and had the feeling that whatever it was knew that she was watching them. She called her dog back, which had been off the leash, and she then hurried away, back towards the dark footpath that leads up towards Meadow Drive, and she tried to not look back. Kim said that she never walked her dog alone on the golf course again after that eerie experience.

Kim's witness account fascinated me because of its similarities to other sightings around the Bude area, both inland and out at sea, but also because I used to walk my dog (Geordie) on the golf course in the early hours of the morning too, and I sometimes felt that there was an odd energy to certain areas of the golf-course. Geordie, as with most dogs, was very sensitive to energies, there were places that he just would not go, and one of them was on that same footpath up behind Meadow Drive, the other was at a particular spot on the high cliffs between Crooklets Beach and Northcott Mouth, places where suicides are known to have taken place, including one of a lovely lady that I knew through my involvement with Bude Rugby Club many years ago.

Jo's Story

This next witness testimony fits in well with Kim's experience on the golf course. About twenty years ago, at around 9:00 pm on a clear summer's evening, Jo, an old friend of mine, along with a friend of hers, both witnessed several fast moving lights heading in from the sea towards Summerleaze Beach at Bude. They watched mesmerised as the lights came towards them at considerable speed, wondering what they might be. As they got closer she said they looked like little silver balls. These silver balls, apparently only about the size of a football, had suddenly stopped dead, and then done an amazing sharp 90 degree left turn, (to her right) and travelled at incredible speed in the direction of Crooklets Beach, and then onwards in the direction of the GCHQ top secret government base at Cleave Camp, until they could no longer be seen. I have often wondered if those small silver craft, perhaps drones, were actually aware of, and headed for, the GCHQ base.

Bude's Ghost Trains
Chapter Six

Bude is a small town near the eastern end of the north coast of Cornwall, it has been a popular tourist destination since Victorian times; when it was mostly steam engines that brought the tourists down to Bude. The first steam engines puffed their way in to Bude in 1898 when the railway track and station buildings were run by the London and South Western Railway. It was a busy station for both freight and commuter passengers; many thousands of travellers alighted there for their summer holidays. During its peak operations it was supplying a service to and from London, the journey either way took just under five hours. Sadly, the infamous Dr Beeching consigned Bude Railway Station, and many others like it around the U.K., to history, when he swung his unpopular 'axe' on the third of October, 1966. The railway tracks were quickly removed, and the station house and engine sheds were demolished soon afterwards. All that now remains of the once proud Bude Railway Station is one solitary ivy-covered gate post, and there is a small modern senior citizen housing estate built on the site of the old station.

After putting out an appeal for witnesses to supernatural activity, in and around the Bude area, I received a call from Petra, and she told me a fascinating story which had two corroborating witnesses. In some odd way that our current level of science can't yet explain, it seems that over 50 years after the last steam driven train departed Bude Railway Station, a station that no longer exists, ghostly steam trains are apparently still arriving and leaving!

Petra lived on Bulleid Way, the senior citizens' housing estate which lies on the site of the old Bude Railway Station, situated between Bude Rugby Club, and the main road access in to Bude. The name Bulleid is derived from Oliver V.S. Bulleid, CBE, he was once the Chief Mechanical Engineer for the English Southern Railway; he developed steam engines that were once a part of the fabric of everyday life in Britain.

Petra is in her late 60s now, mentally able, and physically fit. She likes to keep herself busy socially around the town, enjoys spending time with her grand-children, knitting, and doing creative arts. Shortly after she moved in to her retirement bungalow on Bulleid Way, she had begun to see fleeting glimpses of odd people walking by the front of her home. They looked strange, their clothing out of place, they wore the fashions of earlier eras, the 1960s, or perhaps even earlier. The men she glimpsed appeared to be wearing smart business suits, and they usually seemed to be carrying brief-cases and umbrellas.

Petra was curious about these unusual people wandering around her estate, she knew they didn't live there. When she spotted them she'd swiftly put her knitting down, jump up from her armchair, and rush to the front bay window, to get a better look at them, but as soon as she got to the window they had always seemingly disappeared in to thin air, with nowhere that they could possibly have gone in such a short space of time. Petra was also frequently woken up in the early hours of the morning, usually between three and five am, by the sounds of what sounded like steam engines, and people loudly hailing each other. She could never quite make out what the voices were saying, but she said it was reminiscent of a "hectic railway station, with the busy atmosphere of porters, passengers, drivers and guards." Petra remembered a similar 'soundtrack' from her childhood days in the 1950s, when she had lived quite near Waterloo Railway Station in South London. There was an olfactory element to her strange experiences too, as Petra sometimes experienced the smell of the steam engines too, a very distinctive aroma that she had clearly recognised.

One day Petra was out in her front garden, chatting to two new neighbours. Sally and Joan had recently moved to Bude from what Cornish people call 'up-country,' which basically means anywhere east of the Tamar River! During the course of their conversation, Sally had asked Petra a question that had been playing on her mind: "Do you know where Bude's railway station is?" Petra responded by telling her that it used to be where they were now stood, all around them, before the Bulleid Way Estate was built, and she went on to explain how the station buildings had been demolished back in 1966, when the line was closed by Dr Beeching's cuts. Sally had looked surprised, having expected to hear a different response, something more like: "Oh, it's a mile or so away, but the sound carries at night." Sally explained to Petra why she had asked, saying that she had been hearing the sounds of steam trains, whistles, and loud male voices calling out to each other, during the early hours of the morning. Joan, intrigued by the conversation, had then opened up to Sally and Petra about her own very similar experiences. Petra had, up until that conversation with her two new neighbours, always kept her weird steam engine experiences to herself, but she now opened up about her own ghostly steam engine experiences. She said she was quite relieved, to know that she wasn't the only one who was hearing them, during the early hours of the morning.

Whilst researching this chapter I came across two other steam engine cases which particularly intrigued me, as each of them had a connection to the experiences of the three ladies on Bulleid Way. The author, Joan Rendell, of Launceston, told Michael Williams, "I took my car down to Truscott's Garage in Launceston, to have its annual MOT." (The garage is on the site of the old disused Launceston Railway Station.) "While I was waiting for the Truscott mechanics to check my car over, I decided to take Zeus, my dog, for a walk on the old railway track-bed in the direction of Egloskerry. We walked for about half a mile, and then we turned back towards Launceston. As I was walking back, I distinctly heard a steam train coming towards us from the direction of Egloskerry. It had felt so real that I instinctively pulled Zeus up on to the grass verge with me, and then looked back to watch the train coming, even though I knew there were no tracks, and it wasn't possible for there to have been a train coming! The sound of the phantom train got closer and closer, getting colder the closer it came to us, it was so eerie! As we say in Cornwall, it gave me quite a turn."

Joan went on to say, that shortly after that creepy experience, John, a friend of hers, and John's friend, Doug, both of them railway enthusiasts, had called on her at her home in Launceston. Doug had tagged along with John because he had wanted to meet Joan, to get an autographed copy of 'Hawker Country', a book that she had recently written about the Rev. R.S. Hawker. Shortly after having a cup of tea and biscuits together, and Joan signing the book for Doug, the two men had left to go to look around the old, and now abandoned railway stations of Tresmeer and Otterham, which were both once on the same Southern Railway route that had included Launceston, Egloskerry and Bude.

A few days later John rang Joan. He wanted to thank her for her hospitality, and tell her that they had both really enjoyed reading her new Hawker book, but also wanted to tell her about something really odd that had happened to him, and their mutual friend Doug, whilst they were on the site of the old Tresmeer Railway Station. "You know where the curve is by the arch at Tresmeer Joan? Well, we'd just walked along there, and we were talking about the railway, when we both stopped and looked around. I was puzzled, I said to Doug, "Do you hear what I can hear?" Doug replied, "Yes John, I do, and if there were still rails here I'd swear I could hear a train coming!" Joan, as with Petra in the previous experience, had now been emboldened to share her own strange steam train experience, and so she told John what she had experienced on the old track-bed near Launceston.

As a small post-script to this chapter, I will tell you about a conversation I recently had in connection to these strange steam train occurrences in North Cornwall, and indeed elsewhere around the world. I was chatting to some open-minded friends of ours about my research in to ghostly steam engines. That had pretty soon led us down the path to tales of ghostly inanimate objects, which I have encountered a few times. I made the remark that it's easy to accept that people, and even animals, can have souls, and therefore, by extension, they are capable of haunting, but many people have also encountered ghost planes, trains, auto-mobiles, cyclists, buildings, and landscapes, and frequently combinations of two or more! So my question to our friends was this, "Can a man-made object, such as a train for example, have a soul?" I was interested in their thoughts on the matter. The answer was immediate, and in the affirmative, "But of course!" Our friends are animists you see, and they were surprised that I should even ask the question, as in their world-view it just seems so obvious, that it seemed odd to them that I even asked the question! I then went on to make the comparison of a working steam engine as being similar to the workings of a human body.

My dad, who had spent several years working on the footplate of English Southern Railway steam engines, often intimated that steam engines were living, breathing machines. He wasn't, despite having at least one supernatural experience himself, particularly interested in the paranormal, but at some deeper level I think he understood that material objects can have a life-force. Stephen King, in a much more macabre way, explored similar ideas in his book 'Christine,' which told the story of a possessed 1958 Plymouth Fury auto-mobile.

After pondering what may be going on here on the site of the old Bude Railway Station, and on other disused railway lines, and their associated infrastructure, I have come up with some ideas. These include the possibility of different time-lines running parallel, like the railway lines themselves, and maybe somehow the metaphorical 'signalman of the universe' has accidentally pulled the lever to run one line into another! Another possibility, could be that the strongest of human emotions may travel on the rail tracks, including those of fear and excitement, perhaps powered by electro-magnetic energy that has built up over the years, created by that endless repetitive motion, of thousands of steel train wheels rolling on the rails, which then ultimately may create an unknown field effect. This field effect could be the explanation for so many supernatural experiences that occur on, and around railway lines, and railway infrastructure, including those railway lines that are now disused.

A Southern Railway steam engine at the old Bude Railway Station, looking suitably ghostly, sometime before 1966, on the site where the Bulleid Way housing estate now stands.

Rob and the Puzzling Pottery Pieces

Chapter Seven

Nick was a good friend to so many people in the Bude and Stratton district of North Cornwall, up until his premature death, just a few years ago; he was only in his late 50s. Six feet tall and barrel chested, Nick was a real bear of a man, not a giant as such, but a big man that you would mess with at your peril. Had he have been around in 1643, at the English Civil War Battle of Stamford Hill, just a short walk from where Nick lived and socialized, I'm sure he would have cut an imposing, flamboyant dash, as a Cavalier soldier on horse-back, with his wavy long brown hair, luxuriant moustache, and bushy eyebrows.

I wasn't one of Nick's closest friends, as I had only met him a few years before his untimely demise, but I suspect that Nick made every friend feel, as I did, that they were his best friend. I worked with him on the Royal Mail at Bude for a couple of years, and he greeted me most mornings as if he hadn't seen me in many years. He would occasionally pass by behind me, whilst I was sorting my mail, and as he did so he would playfully slap my back by way of greeting. I have to admit that there were times when I was unprepared, having not seen the big man coming, and the power of that friendly slap would sometimes face-plant me in to my work-frame; he had strong arms, and hands the size of shovels! Nick knew what he was doing, quietly sniggering as he walked away; always the cheerful joker in the pack.

After spending a few minutes in Nick's jovial company my day was somehow always lifted. He often had a joke for his mates, and when Nick told his stories all other conversations in the sorting office would temporarily be put on hold, as everybody quietly tuned in to Nick's deep bass North Cornish tones. Like a droll teller of old; he knew how to tell a good yarn. Nick had that indefinable charisma that only a minority of lucky people possess, he had great presence. When I left the Royal Mail, in the spring of 2007, I no longer saw Nick on a daily basis, but I would still bump in to him in Bude from time to time, usually when I was in town grabbing a pasty at lunchtime. We would laugh and joke, exchange the usual pleasantries, and spend a few happy minutes catching-up, before getting on with our respective days. When I heard the sad news of Nick's death I was shocked, and thinking about it later that night I had found myself tearing up. For a long time I found it difficult to accept, still half-expecting to see Nick around the town. Once you pass fifty, this begins to happen with increasing frequency, (hearing about your friends dying) you begin to realize how fleeting our time here is; it reminds us of our own mortality. As the Cornish comedian Jethro says at the close of his live shows: "Treat every day on earth as if it's your last, one day you will be right."

I ran a small gardening business for many years, and once did a big turfing job for Nick. I spent a couple of lovely hot summer days up at his Stratton property, working on a new lawn, Nick keeping us supplied with cups of tea and stories. The bloke who helped me on that job was my friend Rob, and it is Rob that we have to thank for the strange, but ultimately hopeful story that will soon follow.

After Nick's funeral service many of his closest friends went to the King's Arms for a beer, or several, to celebrate Nick's life. The Kings is a 17th Century pub in Stratton village, just a mile or so inland from Bude on the North Cornwall coast. It was one of Nick's regular haunts, and, as will soon be revealed, it may still be. My friend Rob was among those old friends gathered at the King's Arms that day. Nick had also been a much loved patron at The Tree Inn, just a short walk uphill from the Kings. The Tree Inn is even older than the King's Arms, as parts of it date back to the 13th

Century, is renowned for its close association to the Cornish Giant, Antony Payne, who often drank in there with his own mates, indeed, there is a huge mural of Antony in the Tree Inn's internal courtyard.

Most nights, ever since he was a young man, Nick would have been at one of those two pubs, and frequently probably both, propping the bar up, having lively, friendly conversations and debates, with locals and visitors alike. Nick worked very hard at his Royal Mail job, it entailed starting work at around 4:30 am, and finishing at around 1:00 pm. He would have stood at his frame sorting the mail (each postie has their own frame on which to build up their daily postal round) for at least four hours, and would have then walked many miles delivering the mail for another four to five hours. Apart from the physical energy that was required, there was also the mental attention needed for constantly reading addresses, and putting them in to the right slots on his frame, and later in to the individual letter-boxes. The result of all that hard work, mental and physical (I know because I did it for a while) was that Nick would have got very weary, and would have required forty winks in the afternoons to recover; but he most likely never got it. There were many posties at Bude who worked on at other jobs in the afternoons, some were gardeners, others plumbers or decorators, but Nick preferred to do 'overtime' at the Royal Mail sorting office, which had entailed going out collecting mail from the letter boxes around the town, in one of the Royal Mail's iconic little red mail vans.

On leaving the Kings, or the Tree, at closing time after an evening drinking session, Nick would have wended his way up Union Hill towards his home in Stratton, a fairly strenuous walk of around 15/20 minutes, and perhaps much longer if he had consumed a few too many beers and couldn't walk entirely straight! The hill is steep and winding, and so, on warmer evenings, with the beer and the tiredness possibly combining to create a kind of 'perfect storm,' Nick would have sometimes taken a few minutes breather on the way up, at a particularly well placed public bench. Nick would have got himself a little bit too cozy perhaps, and, occasionally, so I'm told by those who knew him best, he fell asleep!

On one of those occasions, so more recent local Bude and Stratton legend has it, two Bude policemen were driving up Union Hill in their patrol car, in the early hours of the morning. They had noticed Nick, fast asleep on that bench, laying on his back snoring. The kindly coppers, who knew Nick quite well, had gently prodded him with their truncheons to rouse him from his sleepy slumbers, and then, exhaustingly for them, half-dragged the big man in to their police patrol car, to take him home to his wife. On arrival at Nick's home, with the help of Nick's wife, they had laid him down on the sofa in the front room, and had then left, most likely to go up to the Bude Trading Estate, to prepare to catch the workers speeding home after their night-shifts. Nick's wife, after saying 'thank-you' to the kindly coppers, had thought it best to leave her man on the sofa to sleep it off, and had then returned upstairs to her bed. I'm told that about an hour or so later Nick's wife went downstairs to check that Nick was OK, only to discover that he had gone! No, he hadn't been abducted by a UFO, apparently Nick had woken up then taken the short walk back to his favourite bench, to finish off the kip that the helpful cops had so rudely interrupted earlier!

But that lifestyle never stopped Nick from getting up early to go to work, he was always punctual, and happily prepared for more hard graft. I will stress here too that Nick was NOT an alcoholic, yes, he over worked himself, and yes, he probably didn't eat that well, but the beer had mostly made him drowsy, not drunk. Nick could handle his beer, I know that because we were once the last two blokes standing at the Carriers Inn in Bude, one Christmas Eve, well over ten years ago, after a very boozy, happy afternoon and early evening. Nick had been visibly tired, but not drunk, and he had sunk several pints of strong Cornish beer. Nick's drinking habits are very relevant to this story, as you will soon see. I'll hand you over now to my old friend Rob, to finish telling this story in his own way, after all, he was actually there at the celebratory wake at the King's Arms, sadly I wasn't.

"Some say that the recently departed are still amongst their loved ones here on earth, for a short while after their bodily death. An event regarding a dear friend of mine, Nick, certainly bears that out, even to the extent that he actually made himself known to his friends after his death. Following the funeral service both of the Stratton pubs where Nick used to drink and socialize were very, very busy; full to the brim with his friends paying their last respects. I was in the King's Arms with his closest mates, blokes who had, in a few cases at least, known Nick for at least 40 years. We were all having a good time, although the event was obviously tinged with sadness, we were all drinking together and trading our memories of Nick."

Author's Note: Above the pub's front wooden sash windows, with the busy Bude to Holsworthy road just outside, there was a pelmet-shelf, used for decorative pub bric-a-brac, adorned with various items, such as brass tankards and dusty darts trophies. There were also a set of three ceramic plates on that shelf, these were intermittently spaced out along the length of the shelf, with the other items interspersed between them, and all three of those plates had old rhymes inscribed on to them.

Rob: "Gradually, the Kings began to get a bit quieter, many of the punters in the pub had now gone home, there were only a few of us left now, his oldest mates, some of us who had known him since junior school days, we were all sat around the one big table, or, I should say, several smaller tables that had been hastily pushed together earlier. There was only one other person in the pub now, and that was Gina, the Landlady. She was quietly beavering away, washing up glasses, polishing the bar, doing that sort of thing, when suddenly, and for no apparent reason (as there was no traffic or people passing by the pub to have caused it) one of the three plates above the window had come off the window pelmet-shelf. It had appeared to move slightly outwards in to the air, off and away from the shelf, hovering ever so briefly, before it had come crashing down on to the old granite flagstone floor, smashing in to a few pieces.

Somehow I just knew that the crashing plate had something to do with my old mate Nick that he was just letting us know that he was there with us in the pub, listening in to the stories that we were telling about him, enjoying the banter, wishing he was still there with us in body. I'll bet he was laughing at our shocked reaction to the sudden commotion, he would have enjoyed that. One of my mates, possibly Luke or George, suggested that it might have been Nick who knocked it off the shelf, perhaps a bit pissed off with us because he could no longer join us for a beer. I looked around, half expecting to see Nick's smiling face bearing down on us, and see his massive fist hammering the table, we all laughed nervously; a cold chill passed right through me.

Gina, hearing the crash and seeing the pieces of broken pottery on the granite floor, had come out from behind the bar to sweep up the plate debris. I put my beer glass down, got up from my seat, and went over to the broken pottery pieces too, at first it was just to help Gina, but I then had this gut feeling, call it a hunch if you like, to ask her to wait whilst I inspected the bits of pottery on the floor. Gina had stood back, visibly baffled by my strange request, her impatient dustpan and brush hanging by her sides at the ready. I knew there were different old comic rhymes on each of those three dusty plates above the pub window, as only a few weeks previously I had read them all whilst supping a quick half-pint at lunch-time, between my gardening jobs. One rhyme had something to do with not stealing, another one had to do with being faithful to your wife, and the third one was something to do with drinking; but which one of them had fallen? I didn't want to look up at the shelf to see which one was missing, I like to figure things out, I wanted to work it out from the bits of broken pottery on the granite flagstone floor.

There were about eight or nine broken pieces of plate pottery. I painstakingly began to piece them all together, like a kid doing a jigsaw, to see if I could work out the puzzle. The lads, seeing what I was doing, were puzzled and humoured by my strange actions, they came over with their beers and just stood in a circle around me and Gina, watching intently, confused as to why I wasn't just chucking the broken bits in to Gina's dustpan, and getting the next round of beers in. After some early mistakes, trying to fit the wrong pieces together, I began to smile as the plate slowly came back together on the granite flagstones in front of me. I began to hear a slow murmur, a ripple of understanding was beginning to catch on amongst the lads, and Gina too, as the realization of the words in the rhyme that were being reassembled had caught on. These were the words, and I think, well we all thought really, and that they were very relevant to our dear old departed mate Nick. That would have been the plate, the one that he would have grabbed off the shelf and thrown on to the floor, if he had wanted to let us know that he was still there with us in the pub, and, more importantly, that life does indeed go on after death:

'*He who has a drink has another one,*
He who has another one gets
drunk,
He who gets drunk sleeps,
He who sleeps does no sin,
He who does no sin goes to
heaven,
So let's all get drunk and go
to heaven!'

I wish to thank my old friend Rob for sharing his experience of that eventful afternoon in the Kings, I really appreciate it. In loving memory of our mutual friend, Nick, I'm sorry I missed your farewell drinking session at the Kings Nick, we all miss your company, stories and wit, please save me and Rob a place at the bar in Heaven, if we ever make the grade; mine's a Tribute!

Nick was not his real name, and many will know who he really is, I won't say 'was' as I believe that we all live on, and that's what Nick was trying to tell us at the King's Arms that night. I changed his name to protect his family's privacy. I hope that they, and his many friends, enjoy this story and are not offended. I loved the bloke, he was one of my favourite Bude and Stratton characters. I think, had Nick have been raised in Stratton a few hundred years earlier, he would have been a drinking buddy of the great Antony Payne, the famous Stratton giant who fought at the Battle of Stamford Hill. (I'll tell you about BIG 'Tony' in the next chapter). Maybe, after a few pints of good strong Cornish ale at the Tree, they would have good-naturedly arm-wrestled together in the pub's courtyard, now that would have been something to witness; and I wouldn't have wagered against Nick, he was a powerful man too!

The King's Arms, in Stratton

Antony Payne, a Cornish Giant

Chapter Eight

Antony Payne, known to his fellow villagers as 'Uncle Tony' (uncle being an old Cornish term of respect) was born in Stratton, near the eastern end of the north coast of Cornwall, in 1612. Even as a young lad, Antony was already bigger than most adults around him, and his feet were said to be so big that locals had a saying, if they wanted to express how long something was, they would say, "It was as long as Uncle Tony's foot!" Antony, at his young adult peak, measured 7ft 4ins tall, and he weighed in at a massive 32 stones (448 lbs). There are many old North Cornish stories about Antony's immense strength when he was a younger man. One of those stories tells of how he carried two friends up a very steep sea-cliff, just for a wager, he had a friend tucked under each of his huge arms!

He soon became the chief retainer and bodyguard of Sir Beville Grenville of Stowe, (a few miles from Stratton) a leading Royalist Colonel. Antony fought alongside Sir Beville at several English Civil War battles, they were Braddock Down, Modbury and Sourton Down, prior to having to fight in his home-town of Stratton, in May 1643. Two months after the Battle of Stratton Hill (later named Stamford Hill), Antony and Sir Beville once again fought together against Cromwell's forces, but alas, it was to be for the last time, at the Battle of Lansdown in Somerset, where his beloved master, Sir Beville Grenville, died in action.

It is thought that the sight of the giant Antony Payne, leading a ferocious charge up Stratton Hill to attack the Parliamentarians was just too much for the enemy; many had understandably panicked, dropped their weapons, and ran for their lives. There was an old local rhyme in the

Stratton/Bude area for many years after that battle, perhaps it's still chanted by school-boys today:

"His sword was made to match his size, as Roundheads did remember; and when it swang t'was like the whirl of windmills in September!"

Antony was not just a strong man, he was also known to be intelligent, gentle, amusing, loyal and brave, and his daring do exploits had soon gained him the attention of King Charles, who ordered that Antony's portrait (now hanging in The Royal Cornwall Museum) should be painted by the official court artist, Sir Godfrey Kneller, an honour usually only bestowed upon the rich and famous. After the restoration of the throne, seventeen years later, Antony's bravery and loyalty to the crown was remembered and recognised by Charles II, who honoured Antony with the role of 'Halbadier,' a royal guard, armed with a vicious, long shafted axe-like weapon.

On the anniversary of Charles I's beheading, there were some who practised an annual, gruesome, cruel mockery of his memory. They would serve up a calf's head for dinner, in a William and Mary dish. On one such occasion, Antony Payne was present, and, still having loyalty for Charles, had taken exception to the slur, so much so, that he threw the dish, with its macabre contents, out of the nearest window in his rage. A big row soon ensued, which resulted in Antony and the officer responsible for the calf's head dish, having a sword duel at daybreak. It was a fine contest, as the antagonist was an experienced soldier, but Antony's superior strength, and, no doubt, his 'windmill' sword blows, eventually won the day. Antony ran through his opponent's sword arm to disable him, and, as the sword skewered his foe, Antony had exasperatedly shouted, "There's sauce for your calf's head!" But perhaps the most famous Stratton Giant story was this one:

After the Battle of Stratton Hill, as around 300 enemy dead lay strewn all around them, Antony Payne had asked his men to dig 30 trenches, all of them he instructed, to be large enough to hold ten bodies each. When the men had finally done this back-breaking task, they had begun to bury the enemy dead. Nine Parliamentarian corpses were laid in to the first trench. Sweating, filthy, blood-soaked, tired Royalist soldiers, with shovels in hand and blisters already forming, had been awaiting the tenth body to be laid alongside his dead Parliamentarian comrades. Antony Payne was arriving with the tenth man to fulfil his own set quota. As Antony neared the trench, the supposedly dead Royalist under his arm had weakly pleaded with the giant holding him, saying: "Surely you wouldn't bury me yet sir, before I have breathed my last?" Antony Payne, and I'll give him the benefit of the doubt here, was surprised to see that the Royalist soldier was still alive. He had looked down at the feeble, half-dead man drooping weakly under his arm, and had responded, "I tell thee, our trench was dug for ten, and there's only nine men in it so far, so I'm sorry, but you have to join your comrades." "But I'm not dead yet," the man had begged and pleaded with the huge man holding him like a soon to be discarded piece of rubbish. (I wonder if the Monty Python team who wrote 'The Holy Grail' had heard this story.) "I haven't done enough living yet! Please have mercy on me sir, don't hurry a poor fellow into the earth before it's his time." After a very unnecessary, long, cruel pause, and no doubt a smirk or two shared with his Royalist mates, Antony Payne slowly responded, "I won't hurry thee man, I will put thee down quietly on the ground with those who may recover from their wounds, and I'll cover thee up, and there thee canst die at thy own leisure."

Antony Payne, fortunately for the poorly Royalist soldier, was only messing with him, and he did not forget him. After the mass burials were completed, Antony had apparently walked over to the dead and dying soldiers at the side of the battlefield, to find him. Having eventually found the man, still breathing weakly under an old blood-soaked blanket, he had smiled and winked at him. Lifting him up from the ground, he had thrown him over his enormous shoulder, then walked off down the hill towards his little cottage in Stratton, where he continued to care for the wounded Parliamentarian soldier, until he had fully recovered.

During my research on Antony Payne, I was reading a book written in 1870 by the multi-talented, eccentric vicar of nearby Morwenstow, the Rev R S Hawker. He clearly had a deep interest in local history, legends and folklore, and wrote with great enthusiasm about the Battle and Antony Payne in particular, he mentions, in passing, that the Parliamentarian soldier who Antony saved from the grave that terrible day, had descendants still living in Stratton village.

When Antony Payne passed away, many years later, in 1691, at his home in Stratton, his coffin was too large to move up and down the stairs of his cottage. His friends had to cut a huge hole in the first-floor oak floor beams, and then lower him down to the ground floor with ships' ropes and pulleys borrowed from nearby Bude. The local Stratton lads had then taken it in turns, to carry their old friend Antony over to St Andrew's Church graveyard, to lay him to rest in the consecrated ground.

Antony Payne, the Stratton Giant, 1612-1691

The Runaway Stallion of Poughill Road

Chapter Nine

It's a very short drive from Stratton Church, where, in 1691, we've just left Antony Payne, the Stratton Giant, to rest in the graveyard, to go to our next location. We will pass by the site of that hideous historic English Civil War battle on our way, (which we discuss some more soon) and an ancient crossroads. My lad Dexter told me about a creepy experience that he'd had, about ten years ago, during the early hours of a May morning, just on the Bude side of the Poughill Road. Dex had just walked down through the deathly quiet village, with its 13th Century church and ancient white cob-walled thatched cottages, when he'd distinctly felt an unseen presence following along slightly behind him, over to his left, behind the high banked Cornish hedge at the side of the road. The creepy experience had so unnerved him that he never walked that way home again.

My witnesses to another weird event, in exactly the same area, are Len and Lydia, but mostly Len. Their creepy experience happened while they were living in the top half of an ancient white-washed cob-walled cottage. Their first floor flat, from where Len would see the strange events unfolding from a wooden first floor window, was situated directly above the old Poughill Post Office and a little convenience shop, now sadly both long gone.

Firstly, here's a little local geography to set the scene, if you go left from their old cottage, uphill on the Poughill Road, it will take you towards the Inch's Shop Crossroads, (where I had a weird encounter, but more on that later) and if you were to go right, downhill, it will take you through where Dex was followed by a strange presence, towards Flexbury, another district of Bude. Len and Lydia's first-floor part of the cottage was right on the tee-junction where the Northcott Road, coming up from where Grenville is situated, meets the Poughill Road. As I've tried to show, quite a few of the strange experiences that were submitted to me for this book took place around this 'Bude Triangle.' We'll let Len pick up his own story up from here:

"It was one late, balmy, summer evening, back in the mid-1970s. My wife Lydia and I were living in a small flat above Poughill Post Office, on a very quiet, rural tee-junction. We had only been there for about two months at the time. It was still very hot, after a beautiful day, so we had all the windows wide open. We were watching something on the television, when we both started to hear what at first sounded like a baby screaming. Then it eventually stopped, for about half an hour.

By this time Lydia had gone on to bed, but I had decided to stop up, as I had got interested in a film I had begun to watch. That's when the screaming began again. I was curious so I turned down the television volume so I could hear the strange sound more clearly. I wondered what the hell was going on. I decided to turn the television off, and then stuck my head right out of the first floor window, to see if I could work out from where the noise was coming. The screams just got louder and louder, and closer and closer, it was incredible. It was hellish. I stayed there in the window, peering intently up the road, waiting for whatever it was to finally show itself, if and when it would finally arrive just beyond St Olaf's Church up to my left. I was straining my eyes, and the sound was just so damn eerie. That's when I first saw a glow beginning to appear just up by the church, and that glow just got bigger, and brighter, and the screaming sounds intensified in to a terrible, unearthly screeching. The sound was just so piercing! Then this glowing thing passed right under me in the narrow lane beneath my window. It was like a big shining ball, with what looked like comet-like streaks flaring out of the rear. It flew past me doing about 30 to 40 miles an hour. The sound as it passed me was absolutely incredible, difficult to express in mere words, it was an amazing, but very scary experience. As it passed by I turned my head, fascinated by what I was witnessing, to watch where this glowing thing would go. Instead of just continuing on, straight down the road towards the Flexbury area, it went off slightly to the right just after it passed our cottage, straight through the red GPO telephone kiosk, then on through the big stone wall that was behind it. Then it was gone, but presumably it would have continued on through the garden behind that high wall, I don't know, you can't see that from the window. I have to admit that the experience really shook me up. I staggered backwards from the window in shock, then ran, somewhat unsteadily, in to the bedroom. I dived in to our bed and stayed there awhile under the bed covers! Lydia was worried by my strange actions, she asked me what the hell I was doing. I tried to explain to her what I had just heard and seen, but I struggled to speak as I was so shook-up.

We never spoke of that night again, well, not until many years later, when we were both in Bude's Summerleaze Beach Hotel. A group of us were at the bar, telling each other our personal creepy stories, and I had gathered up my courage and decided to stand up and tell mine for the first time in public. A friend who was also present got in with his story first, before I could tell mine. I was amazed by the story he told, as it was eerily similar to what I had experienced seeing and hearing at the cottage. I have never forgotten that night I saw that thing, and I will never walk through that village again after dark, just in case I hear that awful sound again."

Len was referring to the same road where my son Dexter had his creepy experience while walking home through Poughill late one night. Did the following traumatic events, that I am about to relate to you, have any connection to each other, or any bearing on what Dex experienced, on that same country lane around ten years ago, and what Len saw from his cottage window in the 1970s?

In mid-May, 1643, at the height of the English Civil War, the Royalist forces, (2,400 men) under the command of Sir Ralph Hopton, had arrived in Bude, setting up camp on Summerleaze Downs, somewhere near where the present day Sainsburys store now stands, having ridden or walked up from Launceston, the ancient capital of Cornwall. They would, on the following day, on their way to do battle, pass, if not through Poughill village, then very close by, and later, during and after the battle, fleeing men and horses may well have retreated through the village too, but more on that later. They gathered together that night on Summerleaze Downs, to rest and prepare for the battle they were expecting to fight the next day.

The Royalist leaders were concerned that the Parliamentarians, under the command of Henry Grey, the Earl of Stamford, who had set up camp on Stratton Hill, just outside Stratton village, out-numbered their forces by at least two to one, and would also soon be receiving cavalry reinforcements from the south. They therefore decided to push on, to engage the enemy as quickly as possible, before the enemy forces could be increased.

Four columns, of 600 Royalist soldiers each, including the Stratton Giant we discussed in the previous chapter, Antony Payne, began to leave Summerleaze Downs at first light, in order to attack the enemy forces from three different directions. As they marched towards the Parliamentarian defenders they were being joined by many Royalist supporting men from the Bude and Stratton areas. They found it tough going, as the 5,600 Parliamentarians on Stamford Hill were putting up a brave, stubborn resistance to their constant attacks.

By three in the afternoon the Cornish Royalists had almost run out of ammunition, and were thrown back by a vicious pike attack, but they had then miraculously rallied, very likely under the local leadership, and inspiration of the Stratton giant, as discussed in my short chapter on the Stratton giant, to deliver a really ferocious Cornish Royalist counter-attack, which had completely taken the Roundhead Parliamentarians by surprise. The Roundheads fell back in total disarray, panicking, running for their lives, leaving behind their canons and other essential equipment too. At this point, Sir Ralph Hopton, sensing final victory, released his Royalist Cavalry to finish off any remaining resistance. Many men, around 300, mostly Parliamentarians, were either killed or terribly wounded that day, and 1700 prisoners were taken by the victorious Royalists. Indeed, it was said that the excessive blood spilt on the battlefield that day, by men and horses, had acted as a fertiliser on the ground that it soaked. There were reports that the land yielded more bushels of barley to the acre for many years after the battle.

It's my guess that many men, and horses, would have panicked amidst the ferocious, clamorous violence of that dreadful day. I wonder if the glowing, shining ball, with the streaks flaring out of the back, and the awful screaming sounds that Len witnessed and heard that May evening, was one of the panicking horses, desperate to get away from the horrendous carnage and noise, and whether the unseen presences that haunt the Poughill Road are perhaps Parliamentarian soldiers who ran away from the terrifying battle, and are perhaps still, on some other level of existence, hiding in the Cornish hedges, fearful of discovery by the Royalist forces. Maybe when we walk down Poughill Road on the May anniversary of the battle, as Dex did, they may be fearful of us, perhaps mistaking us for Royalist soldiers. Maybe they are stuck in that time, unaware that the world has now moved on.

A week or so after I thought I had finished the above chapter, I had an interesting discussion with Shelly, a Welsh friend, about Len's glowing ball, and what it might have been. Shelly and his partner Bella host the thought-provoking, and occasionally amusing, 'Weird, Wacky, Wonderful, Stories Podcast.' Shelly had suggested that the violent, bloody battle may have, via the pain and suffering of the many men and horses that were present, created energetic balls of 'extreme spiritual anguish,' which may occasionally be drawn together in a snowball type effect, to finally erupt, making their presence felt in our physical world on anniversaries of the May 1643 battle, like a paranormal boil being lanced, and this is then perceived by those who are sensitive to such things, people like Len. I think that's as good a theory as any I have heard.

Large dark, drifting, cloudy looking shapes are occasionally seen by witnesses on the Stamford Hill Battle site, perhaps it is Antony Payne, taking a ghostly walk from his resting place in Stratton, to re-visit a traumatic day in his life, or perhaps it could be the shade of Hawker of Morwenstow, who, although not as big as Antony Payne, was known to be very interested in the Battle of Stamford Hill. Dog walkers, with no prior knowledge that there was ever a terrible military clash on the site, have heard the sounds of battle going on all around them, the thunderous noise of canons firing, men shouting, screams of agony, and the screeching sounds of terrified horses panicking, as if they are in the middle of a battle that is still being fought, at least 370 years after the Cornish Royalist forces claimed victory.

One lady witness, who was crossing the old battlefield in May 2010, was absolutely convinced that she had suddenly found herself in the middle of dozens of desperate fighting men, her account sounded fantastic, like a scene from TV's 'Time Tunnel.' The lady said the weird experience lasted around five minutes in all, during which time she had heard the metallic clash of steel on steel, men screaming, groaning, yelling, and, very likely, some good old fashioned English cursing too!

I invite any readers who live near to the Stratton battlefield site, particularly those in the larger, closer detached properties, such as 'Hopton's Rise,' to let me know if they, or anybody else that they know, has ever experienced any strange paranormal activity, on or near the 1643 Stamford Hill battle site. I would love to hear about your experiences. My contact details are listed later in the book, in anticipation, thank you.

Poughill Post Office and the little shop

The site of the Battle of Stamford Hill, as it looks in 2019

"Owls Aren't that Big Mark!"

Chapter Ten

This is the weird personal incident that I alluded to in the previous chapter, which occurred at Inch's Shop Crossroads, just above Poughill village, and fairly close to Stratton's 1643 Stamford Hill Battle site. Crossroads have long been recognized and associated as places of natural power, utilized by Pellers (magic practitioners) to enhance spell-work, or they may have had some kind of diabolical significance, as in the story of the blues guitarist, Robert Johnson, who was alleged to have met the devil at a crossroads. Judging by the quantity of witness accounts to anomalous events around this area, that flowed in to my in-box a few years ago, when I publicly requested peoples' weird experiences, the Inch's Shop Crossroads appears to be very close to the geographical centre of an area of ongoing high strangeness; a paranormal cross-hairs of sorts, or, to reiterate what I said in the previous chapter, we could even call it the 'Bude Triangle.'

I had dropped my son Dexter (21 at the time) off at his friend's place in Stratton, earlier that night, he had gone up there to rehearse with his band. "I'll ring you later Dad to let you know when to pick me up," he had said, as he'd grabbed his bass and amp from the back of my car, then slammed the door shut a little bit too hard. Winding down my side window I had replied, "OK, but don't make it too late please Dex, I have to be up early in the morning." "Alright Dad, it won't be, I'll ring you at about 10:30." He'd responded, as he'd walked briskly away, heading towards the illuminated crack of a partially opened garage door, which had been emitting power chords from an electric guitar, and the faintest whiff of a sweet aroma from an illegal substance.

I liked to help my kids get to and from those difficult to get to rural places, where their friends mostly seemed to live, at least that way I knew that they would get home safely, and I could sleep untroubled by worries of them walking home on dark, dangerous, remote lanes in the middle of the night. The Bude area is bordered by the sea to the north, and mostly farming country and villages inland for many miles. It's at least 50 minutes from Barnstaple, a small Devon town to the north, and 90 minutes from Exeter, to our south, the nearest city. Once you are a few minutes away from Bude during the night, the roads are generally much darker than their urban equivalents due to a lack of street lighting. In a recent London University study of light pollution, the North Cornwall area was shown to be amongst the darkest in the whole of the UK, and so, with that in mind, hopefully you can picture the coming scene a little better.

I was sat at home in the Flexbury area of Bude, half-watching TV, and half-reading a book about Horatio Nelson, when, at around 10:30 pm, Dex did ring, "Alright Dad? Come and get me please." "Yes." I said, "No worries Dex, I'll be up there in about ten minutes." I think I may have been a little bit too cozy and warm at home that night, because, somehow, and this was something I had never done before, I must have fallen asleep literally just after taking that call. Strangely I can recall having been fully alert when I took the call. It was so totally out of character. Just plain weird.

The next thing I knew I was being woken up by another telephone call. It was Dex again, but this time he sounded very annoyed, "Where the hell have you been Dad? I've been trying to ring you for two and a half hours!" His angry, loud words took me by surprise, because as far as I was aware, I had only just put the 'phone down from his previous call. I checked my watch. He was right, it was now just before 1:00 am. I had somehow lost two and a half hours. "Oh **** it! I'm sorry Dex, I must have fallen asleep." It had felt strange, but that feeling was over-powered by my feeling bad about making Dex wait, and how awkward that must have been for him. His friend would almost certainly have been kept up far later than he would have wanted, keeping Dex company, and Dex may have been concerned that I had crashed en-route to pick him up. I apologized again, then said, "I'll be up to you in about ten minutes." I had quickly grabbed my car keys from the drawer unit in the hall, opened the front door, then stepped out in to a tranquil Victoria Road. It was a chilly night with a full moon. I hurriedly walked down the road in the direction of Crooklets Beach, as my car was parked just around the corner on Summerleaze Avenue, right outside my friend Dick's Bicycle Repair Shop.

I opened the door of my Suzuki Vitara Jeep, got in, slammed the door shut, started the engine, and roared off in to the night. I didn't anticipate it taking me too long to get up there. I knew I could floor the accelerator, as it was doubtful there would be any police cars out and about at that time in the morning to notice me. The coppers would, I had assumed, either be at home in bed, or, if they were on night duty, hidden away outside Bude's trading estate, where they liked to sit and wait for the night shift lads from Bott's factory to clock-off, as they knew those lads liked to break the speed limit in a rush to get home to their wives and beds. I made rapid progress out on to the Poughill Road, passing through where Len had seen the glowing orb many years earlier, then, with my right foot hard down to the floor, and my holey exhaust waking up everybody in North Cornwall, I went up through Poughill village like a Finnish rally driver in a Swedish forest. I passed St Olaf's Church, almost taking out somebody's home-made jam stand outside their cottage gate, went past the Preston Gate pub, and I was at Inch's Shop Crossroads almost before I knew it.

Inch's Shop may perhaps sound like some kind of a store, but in reality it is now just a simple, quiet, rural crossroads. However, there are many crossroads in Cornwall with the word 'shop' tagged on the end of the name, another example is Box's Shop, this is because there were once small cottages there, which acted as shops to the local land workers, who were 'tied' to their employers. The money the workers earned could only be spent in their employer's shop, a form of servitude that ensured the employer's wages (tokens) were only spent within his shop, thereby constantly recycling the employer's money!

If I'd have gone left, it would have taken me across beautiful coastal rolling fields, and then on towards GCHQ, the top secret British/U.S. government spying facility (where personnel have witnessed a black triangle UFO hovering directly overhead) but I needed to turn right, and head on down past the site of the 1643 English Civil War battle that we discussed earlier, and from there drive on towards the ancient village of Stratton.

I had come to a complete halt at the crossroads, in the very unlikely event that there may have been somebody else out on the country lanes that late too. I had quickly checked to my left for traffic, and, as expected, there wasn't any. Then, when I looked over to my right, there it was, it was just standing there in the middle of the road, slightly over to my right, and it was staring directly at me with mesmerising eyes……………. a GIGANTIC owl!

The owl stood taller than my Suzuki's bonnet, which I would say was around four feet high. I would estimate the owl's circumference, at its head, to have been around eighteen inches, and the top half of its body to be about two feet wide. I decided to wait a moment to see if it would fly away, as I had no wish to drive in to it, but it just continued to stand there, staring directly at me with its inquisitive, penetrating, dark eyes. I had the strangest feeling that it wasn't really an owl at all, but some weird dwarf-like man. Whatever it was he was studying me intensely, and seemed angry, as if I was somehow disturbing him. I had the feeling that there was something hidden away behind him too, that he was shielding something, but all I could see was the outline of the field hedge in the moonlight. I remember pushing the button on my car's door to lower the side window, and then stupidly shouting, "Hey! You, get out of the ****** road!" As if the immense owl would understand not just the English language, but foul English language too. There was still no traffic about, and I decided, seeing as I was already running very late, to just drive very slowly towards it, in the hope that it would be gently coaxed in to moving out of my way. As I did so, the huge owl continued to stare me down, like a bully in the school playground. Then, as I got almost up to him, perhaps about three feet away, he had suddenly taken off and flown towards me, but slightly to my right. I felt the down-draught as he flapped his wings; it actually rocked my car. I had watched in amazement, as the giant owl had flown within inches of my face, its monumental sized head was turned directly towards me; he was still staring inquisitively and threateningly at me as he departed the scene.

I drove on, a bit shaken up by the odd experience, down past the site of the Stamford Hill battle on my left, and then further on down towards Stratton village. Fortunately, I had arrived at the property, where I had dropped Dex off several hours earlier, without any further strange incidents. He was outside the garage, sitting on his amp, smoking the remains of a rollie, impatiently waiting. He looked at me disgustedly, then at his watch, shook his head, got up, stubbed his rollie out on a low garden wall, chucked his gear in the rear of the jeep, got in the front passenger seat, slammed the door shut a little bit too hard, and then, half-grunting, said, 'Alright Dad?' I apologised to Dex again for being so late, and asked him how the rehearsal had gone, then we began the short drive back home. As we drove back through the Inch's Shop Crossroads, I told Dex about the gigantic owl that I had just seen on my way up to get him. "Owls aren't THAT big Dad." was all Dex said, very matter-of-factly. Strangely, it was only then that I thought. 'He's right, owls aren't THAT big.'

I'll admit that I'm no naturalist, and I never watch animal/nature programmes on the TV, I'm probably one of the few people in England who's not in the David Attenborough fan club. To be brutally frank, I'd sooner watch some paint drying. I do, however, enjoy occasionally seeing British wild animals in their natural habitats, I love most of them, well, except for snakes, apologies to St Patrick, but I'd like to send all British snakes over to Ireland on a one-way ticket. But, despite that, I was brought up in the countryside, and I DO know a gigantic owl when I see one, and I definitely DID see one. I shared my owl encounter experience with a knowledgeable friend, a man who probably does enjoy David Attenborough's TV wildlife shows, Derek Thomas. (Derek kindly told me of a few of his own strange experiences for this volume of the book). He listened intently to me recounting the odd event, already reaching out to his bookshelf for his 'Observer Book of British Birds' as I spoke, then said, in his distinctive, masculine black country dialect, "Owls aren't THAT big Mark!"

Well, to cut a long story short, we did some research together on both local and migrant birds, and there weren't any that matched the description of what I had encountered at Inch's Shop Crossroads. Occasionally, large birds are blown off course in to Cornwall whilst migrating elsewhere, there was a recent case of a big bird from South America being seen all over Cornwall, but it wasn't at all owl-like in its appearance. Some people may be wondering if I encountered a blown off-course Giant Eagle Owl, but I doubt it, as they are smaller than what I saw at the crossroads. Apparently there have been sightings of undocumented owl species, said to be somewhere between three and five feet high, and they are comically named 'Big Hoot!' Is it possible that I saw a Big Hoot? Well, it certainly seemed to make some people laugh when I told them about my huge owl experience. The Mescalero Apache tribal legends talk of huge, malicious owls, they were said to mesmerise and paralyse their prey, with intense, scary eyes, and then swallow their victim's whole, including children and small adults. If it had been one of those, at six feet tall and 200lbs I might have been a match for him.

Just recently I heard of another strange owl encounter here in Cornwall, although in this case they were not big owls, just regular British sized owls. They were seen by my friends Barbara and Matt, down in the Penwith area of far western Cornwall. Both witnesses said that the owls definitely appeared to be following them around, over a distance of many miles, which the owls had covered as fast as their cars, turning up again and again, and even waiting ahead of them, before following behind their cars again. Both Barbara and Matt are researchers in to strange phenomena, already very aware of strange owl sightings related to UFOs, and that may have had some bearing on what happened. To paraphrase my own quote in my first book, (Wyatt's Weird World) 'When you seek out strange owls, you shouldn't really be too surprised if strange owls begin to seek you out too.'

What you are about to read in this next section was not planned at all, it is only here, tagged on at the end, because of a very weird synchronicity I experienced. It occurred very shortly after I thought I had finished this owl chapter. After about four hours straight of typing, I finally stopped hitting the keys on the keyboard, and I sat back, fairly satisfied with my work. I needed to give my brain and eyes a rest, so I thought I'd treat myself to a bottle of beer and an interesting podcast. I got the beer from the fridge, then sat down on the sofa to peruse paranormal podcast options on YouTube. I spotted one called 'Expanded Perspectives.' The episodes listed included one where the thumb-nail depicted a picture of the archetypal alien, you know the one, yes, that one, the one with the big almond shaped eyes. The alien was pictured alongside a photo of an owl, and the gaze of that owl pulled me in like metal filings to a magnet, it brought back to me my big owl experience. It was unsettling, but I really felt I needed to listen to that podcast, so I clicked play, sat back, put my feet up on the coffee table, grabbed my beer, and began to listen to the show. Kyle and Cam, the hosts of the Texas based show, soon got my full attention when they began to talk about owls, and the strange connection that they have to the UFO phenomena.

Strangely enough, I had previously ended this chapter with an appeal to anybody who had personally seen, or had any information about, abnormally large owls in Cornwall. It had soon felt as if my appeal was already being answered, somebody, or something, was pointing me in the right direction. Cam was relating a witness testimony from one of their listeners, it was about a huge owl that he'd experienced on a country lane in Texas. Here's the story, and note how similar it is to what I encountered at the Inch's Shop Crossroads near Poughill, in Cornwall, (UK):

> "I was alone in my car, driving down a dark country road at night. I spotted a Giant owl, it was about five feet high, and it was stood at the side of the road in front of me. I slowed right down, unwound the window, and had a good look at it. It didn't fly away. I got a very weird vibe from the owl. It was as if the owl was angry with me, and he wanted me to leave. I drove off feeling confused and scared."

A few days later their Texas witness (a photographer by trade) had apparently gone to photograph an owl's nest near his home. It was only then that the realization had dawned on him, that the thing that he had seen could not have been an owl, as it had been far too big, and besides, his senses, since the event, had increasingly told him that the huge owl was not what it had seemed to be.

The Texas witness decided to seek the assistance of a professional hypnotist, in order to try to access any repressed memories, or subconscious images of his strange experience, that might shed some light on the mystery. The hypnotist who put him under asked him to fully describe the big owl. In his altered state, the witness studied the owl very carefully from top to bottom. As the witness's attention travelled further downwards there had apparently been a long pause. "So, what do you see?" the hypnotist had impatiently asked him, his pen poised over his notebook.

"The owl is wearing……….. red boots!" The witness had nervously replied.

What we need to bear in mind is that modern science suggests that life is all about vibrations and frequencies. Our brains are receiving and decoding signals, and then putting our own independent interpretation on everything that we see. The huge owl that the Texas witness saw, and the one that I saw, may not have been a foreign owl species, or an unclassified owl-like creature, it may have been something else entirely. Perhaps it was something that is capable of projecting an owl-like image on to our brains, as a kind of screen image, as it didn't want us to see it in its true form. It may think it is protecting our sensibilities by shielding the way it really looks. Maybe it projects the image of something it thinks we would see as 'normal' or unthreatening, but perhaps it hasn't yet worked out the concept of scale! I'll just be thankful they didn't choose to project a snake or a rat. Having said that, everything, as I said earlier, is about vibration and frequency, therefore what we see with our eyes is only really our 'best guess' anyway, we are only filling in the gaps.

Mike Clelland, a researcher in to UFOs and associated phenomenon, has extensively studied these large owl encounters, and I recall him speaking of a similar encounter where the witness heard the words, 'Owl, owl, owl, owl, owl, owl' over and over again, like a mantra as he was looking at it. Was that his brain trying to make sense of it, and/or resisting it, or was it, as I've just suggested, the thing that he was looking at sending him the suggestion, in order to disguise itself from the witness?

I recall seeing a magician-illusionist at a horse racing meeting in England, on a TV documentary about magic. The illusionist had backed a horse to win, and it had come in ninth out of perhaps ten horses. No matter, the illusionist showman went back to the betting office and gave the girl his losing betting slip. The girl said, "I'm sorry sir, but you haven't a winner here, your horse finished in ninth place." "Look at me," the magician had quietly responded to the girl in a dull, monotone voice, whilst leaning in close to her, and staring intently in to her eyes. The girl did so, and she soon appeared to be mesmerized. He then said, very slowly and clearly, "This horse did not finish fourth, it finished first, please pay me my winnings." After a short period of staring at the losing betting slip, the confused looking girl said, "Oh, I'm sorry sir, so it did." She then paid out a lot of cash on the losing bet. The magician took the money off her, said, "Thank-you," then he walked away unchallenged. He went back ten minutes later to give the now totally baffled girl the money back. He did not explain to the TV audience how he convinced her of his lie, but I assume it had a lot to do with the power of hypnotic suggestion/memorization techniques, and the clever manipulation of sound frequencies when he spoke. Consider for a moment the mesmeric power that Hitler harnessed in his speeches to the German people, had he mastered the same art, but on a much larger scale? I believe so. Hitler, and some of his closest Nazi colleagues, were known to have had a deep interest in the occult and black magic, but that is a whole other book in itself.

There is often a transformative, portent element to the huge owl sightings too. That is to say that the witness, after they have had the sighting, will perhaps go on to have massive changes in their lives; I know I did, but that is far too private to go in to in any detail here. I'll just say that, in retrospect, my life, and those of my loved ones, after my strange owl sighting, was turned on its head by rapid events that I felt, and still feel, were somehow pre-destined to be, not within my conscious control, for some greater purpose that hopefully may become clearer in the years to come. It's worth checking out Mike Clelland's books as they look in much greater detail at both this strange huge owl phenomena, and their portent effect on witnesses.

Inch's Shop, near Poughill, as it once was

The Haunting of Domesday Cottage

Chapter Eleven

Just a ten minute drive from the Inch's Shop Crossroads, and no more than fifteen from the 1643 Stamford Hill battle site, brings us to this mystery haunted location, somewhere near Sandymouth Beach, an ancient property that was mentioned in William the Conqueror's 1086 Domesday Book. My witnesses are Tom and Jane, who lived there during the 1990s, and the early years of the new Millennium. I have been sworn to secrecy to not give the real name of the cottage, or its exact location away, in order to protect the privacy of the current tenants, and also their landlord who still lives next door, the last thing they might need is hordes of TV ghost-hunters descending on them; especially any who ignorantly taunt spirits. For this recounting of the story we'll just call the cottage 'Domesday Cottage.' This is yet another one of many high strangeness cases that flooded in to my inbox, from an area that I now think of as the 'Bude Triangle.'

On the second of September, 1992, Tom Dell and his wife Jane unsuspectingly moved in to that rental property, here's Tom to tell you their fascinating story in his own words:

"The day we moved in, George, the owner, who lived next door in the other half of the small terraced cottage, was in our side finishing off fitting a new carpet, in readiness for us moving in. I had immediately felt uneasy in the cottage, it had such a heavy, eerie atmosphere. I said to George, "This cottage isn't haunted is it George?" He responded, "Oh, I shouldn't think so Tom," but I wasn't convinced as I kept catching movements out of my peripheral vision, mostly up the stairs to my right. The first real creepy activity that we experienced was the cottage door being knocked, as if somebody was stood outside and wanted us to let them in, and that happened for several nights running. The first time it happened was in the early hours of the morning, I had awoke to some loud knocking, but as I came around it had just gradually faded away. I looked at the alarm clock; it was 3:00 am. The second night I had got up to go to the loo, and on my return to our bed I tried to get back to sleep, but just shortly after I had put my head back down on the pillow, the strange knocking had begun again. I looked at the alarm clock; it was 3:15 am.

We wondered, at first, if the door knocking was George trying to wake us up. Just before we moved in, we had asked him if it would be OK to get a telephone service connected up to the cottage, but George had said, 'No,' because he hadn't wanted telephone cables strewn across his window's view of the sea, but he had quickly added, 'You can give my telephone number to your closest family and friends if you want, just in case they need to contact you in any emergencies, and you can use my telephone too, if you should ever need it,' and so you will understand why we had initially thought it may have been George, coming around to let us know that something awful had happened.

On the third day living at the cottage we had walked in to Bude to do some food shopping, and we were on our way back again. I was carrying some heavy shopping bags. We had just got as far as the Inch's Shop Crossroads, the quiet rural crossroads just above Poughill village (yes, where I saw my huge owl) when it had begun to rain quite heavily; we hadn't gone out prepared with our rain jackets. Jim, Jane's brother, just happened to be coming up the lane from Poughill in his car, he was heading over to see their mum. He stopped alongside us, and he asked if we wanted to go with him. I said, 'No thanks Jim, but thanks for the offer, I'm cold, absolutely saturated, and I just want to get home to run a hot bath,' but Jane said, 'Yes please Jim,' and so she had gone with him to see their mum. I had then carried on walking on my own, back towards Sandymouth and our cottage, getting wetter and colder than ever, it was so miserable, I just couldn't wait to get to the cottage, get my wet clothes off, and have that hot bath.

I eventually got back to our cottage, dripping wet by now, shivering with the cold. I got my key out, opened the cottage door, walked in, and put all the shopping bags down on the stone floor. I then hurried up the stairs, which go up directly in front of the entrance door, to the bedroom and bathroom. I'd only got about half way up the stairs, when there was a very loud, heavy knocking on the front door. Exasperated, I swore under my breath, then shouted, "Yes, alright, I'll be down!" Still grumbling, I turned around and went back down the stairs to open the door; only to find there was nobody stood outside! Now, bear in mind that the very narrow rural lane that connected our terraced cottage to the outside world, was two tenths of a mile long, and it was the only route in to, and out from, our cottages. I peered down the lane, with its high Cornish bank sides, and low over-hanging trees, making it dark and tube-like, and there was nobody in it. I also looked around my neighbour's cottage, and nobody was home. I would have seen, and heard, any vehicle coming and going up that lane, but there were none. I was totally baffled. This all happened at around three in the afternoon, what is it about the third hour of the day and night? I told Jane about the knocking when she returned later, and she was just as baffled.

The cottage was a very small two-storey building, comprising one downstairs sitting room with a tiny kitchen at the back, and one upstairs bedroom, with a small bathroom at the rear. One night in October, 1992, we were both sat on the sofa watching the TV, when we heard the sound of loud knocking coming from under the stairs, which were alongside George's half of the cottage. It was an open staircase boarded out with plywood sheets.

We looked at each other, and both of us said, almost simultaneously, "What was that?" The next thing we know we hear the sound of gravel being thrown at the other wall, which made us both jump up in shock! Then, following quickly on, we heard, coming from the kitchen, the very distinctive sound of a coin dropping in to our electricity coin meter, (in the UK some properties are metered to pay for utilities as required) but there was nobody in the kitchen. These small, odd events, continued through until the latter days of November 1992, and then all the strange events just totally ceased…..well, they ceased until the following October, when, weirdly, all the high strangeness resumed.

One day in early October, 1993, I went up the stairs during the day and was surprised to see a small puddle of water on the stairs. My first thought was that we had a plumbing leak, and so I looked everywhere to check it out, but there was no leak, and no way that we could explain where that water had come from, it was just so strange. Lots of other odd things like that just kept happening too. Small, petty, peculiar things. For example, we frequently heard the unmistakable sound of footsteps going up and down the stairs, and our neighbour George had heard them too, through the adjoining wall, when he knew that we weren't in the cottage. We would often hear what sounded like stones, or marbles, rolling about on the roof too, and Jane's sister and brother-in-law, who were house sitting for us once, heard a loud disembodied deep sigh, it had come from within the sitting room they were sat in! There were also weird coughs, and huge bangs on the wall which made the cottage shake.

(Author's note, along with my son Dexter, and Mezz, a friend of his, at Grenville in 2018, we experienced something very similar in the early hours of the morning, it had felt like something huge had just hit Grenville's walls. I discussed it in my earlier 'Grenville' chapter.)

On another occasion when I was upstairs in the cottage on my own, somebody had called out to me from downstairs, inside the cottage this time, but when I went downstairs to see who it was, of course there was nobody there. Many times I had little stones thrown at me from somebody, or something, in the barn, and my daughter had somebody call out to her, "Hello," from there, almost every time she arrived at the cottage. My niece arrived one morning, and she was surprised to see a lady wearing an old-fashioned bonnet, looking forlornly out of the upstairs bedroom window, out towards the sea, and there were so many other odd sightings and strange incidents too.

One night I went to a gathering I'd seen advertised, at somebody's home near Bude, it was a meeting of a paranormal group called 'Mandala.' I was the new boy there, I didn't know anybody else, having never attended the group before. While I was there I overheard a conversation between a few of the ladies, there was talk of 'rescuing spirits, and sending them off in to the light,' that sort of thing. So I coughed to get their attention, and said to the nearest one, "Excuse me, do you do exorcisms?" The lady smiled, "Well, yes, we do Tom, but we don't like to call it that any more, we prefer to say we do rescue work, why do you ask?" She had long dark hair, a swarthy complexion, wore a lot of jewelry, and in my mind I had immediately thought of her as gypsy-like, her name turned out to be Val, but I have always thought of her as gypsy Val. I told her about all the problems we were having at the cottage, and that I thought we had a resident spirit. She listened carefully to my descriptions of the activities we'd experienced at the cottage, then said, "Oh dear Tom, I don't like the sound of that at all!" I thought, oh, thanks very much, I'm the one who has to live there. It was mid-winter, a very dark, wet evening, and I soon had to go back to the cottage on my own.

By that time we had bought another car, and when I drove home that night I had to drive down that really long creepy lane, it was like driving down a dark tunnel, as the trees and wild hedges on the high Cornish hedge banks completely over-hung the lane. I then had to park my car at the side of the open barn, then walk from there over to the cottage. I was always, by now, expecting to hear voices calling out to me, or have stones thrown at my back. I actually once offered some friends fifty quid (pounds) to walk that long, dark, creepy lane at night on their own, from one end of it to the other, but they all made weak excuses, too scared to accept my challenge.

Val and the other ladies were discussing coming to the cottage to check it out, and I heard them say, "We'll ask Tania to come along with us." I didn't know back then who Tania was, I had no idea.

At that time I'd been suffering from some health issues, which modern pharmaceutical medicine had been unable to help me with, and so I had decided to go down to a spiritualist church in Bude, where they did alternative healing work, to see if they could help me.

When I got there I was greeted by a lovely lady, she said, "Hello, I'm Tania." I immediately had the thought that she was probably the same Tania that the ladies had mentioned, as Bude is a very small community. I said, "Oh, hello Tania, I'm pleased to meet you, I'm Tom, and I believe you're coming to my house soon." Tania looked surprised, and she had responded, "Am I Tom?"

I explained how I'd met the ladies at the Mandala Group, and how they'd mentioned bringing 'Tania' along with them to investigate my Cottage. It was her, she'd not long since taken a call from gypsy Val to request her company to visit a man called Tom, (me) at an old cottage that was experiencing some strange disturbances.

The afternoon the ladies called on us, they had proceeded, with Jane, to walk all around the cottage, barn, and adjoining land. They took loads of notes, and asked us lots of questions. Returning to the cottage later Gypsy Val said, "We've found out a few interesting things for you Tom, firstly, when you answered the door to us earlier, a man ran down the stairs behind you, and he said, "They want me to leave, but I'm not going!" They said he was dressed as if he was from the early 1900s. This was a total surprise to me, as I had no idea that he had been directly behind me when I opened the door. I asked Val and Tania if the spirit was referring to me, and they said, 'No, he's talking about a farmer who once owned the property, when it was a tied-cottage." They explained that there were three spirits haunting the cottage. There was a man, a woman, and a child. They said the woman and child had both died of something that had caused them to have sores and scabs around their mouths, as that's how they had presented themselves to the ladies. We all then discussed what that disease might have been, and we came to the conclusion, given the possible era, and the sores and scabs, that it was most likely small pox. They thought that the mum and the daughter died of the disease, and the man was so distraught to lose them, that he had gone to the barn and hung himself. Val and Tania also saw the spirit of a dog in our cottage, and another woman in the garden. When they mentioned the other woman in the garden my hair had stood on end, as I'd experienced some really weird stuff out there a few times.

I used to pick Jeff (my son) up every fortnight from my ex-wife in Ilfracombe, to spend some time with us at the cottage, or around Bude. We used a part of the garden for growing vegetables, and Jeff had his own little patch there for spuds and runner beans. I was working out there on my own one morning, and I just kept getting the feeling that somebody was watching me, it was very unsettling. That same afternoon I went to get Jeff. When we returned we went out in to the garden to work together.

Jeff was about ten at the time, and we were just quietly working at our separate patches of ground, about thirty feet away from each other, when I suddenly noticed that he was talking to somebody. I couldn't see anybody anywhere near him, so I asked him who he was talking to, and he said, "It's Jane, she's back from work." I said, "Don't be silly Jeff, she's not home yet!" Jeff said, "She must be, she's just been talking to me!" Just as we were having that discussion, Jane suddenly turned in to the long lane, and began the long drive towards us! Jeff looked so frightened and confused, he didn't know what to make of it, and to be honest nor did I.

The ladies did a clearing of Domesday Cottage with sage and incantations - that sort of thing, and to be fair it did feel a lot lighter for a while, but the activity never really fully stopped, especially between October and November of each year of our residency that followed. On the day before we finally left the cottage, in 2004, after twelve years of living there, we packed everything up in to the bedroom, chairs were stacked, crates packed, bags stuffed full of assorted stuff, all that sort of thing. We slept on the sofa downstairs that night, and at about 3 am, we were woken up by an almighty bang, a huge crash, as if somebody had picked up one of the packing crates in the bedroom above, and then thrown it across the room in anger. We quickly went upstairs to the bedroom. I nervously opened the door, expecting to see one hell of a mess, but it was exactly as we had left it, very neat, tidy and organized, absolutely nothing had changed.

Some years later, whilst visiting the Preston Gate Inn in Poughill, I met a lady who used to live fairly near Domesday Cottage. She now lived on the Isle of Wight, but she liked to return occasionally to catch up with her old friends around Bude. When I relayed to her some of the instances of the weird things that had happened to us at the cottage, she had replied, "Oh, I shouldn't be at all surprised about that Tom," she then went on to say that it was always rumoured that a former tenant of Domesday Cottage had hung himself in the barn, after his wife and child had died of small pox."

Hawker and the Caledonian Girl

Chapter Twelve

"At Morwenstow one is not only reaching the end of Cornwall, but it seems the end of the world too." – Sir John Betjeman

Before telling you about my friend Harri's weird encounter in the Bush Inn, I'll first give you a bit of background to this remote corner of North Cornwall. The parish of Morwenstow and the Reverend R.S. (Robert Stephen) Hawker will forever be bound together, and, just as with Cornwall and the Supernatural, I can't really tell the story of one without telling the story of the other.

From our last location, somewhere near Sandymouth Beach, we now have a short, scenic, slight detour, up the North Cornish coast towards Morwenstow, which is the extreme north-eastern area of Cornwall that borders Devon. It's around 8,000 acres of beautiful woodland, fertile fields, Cornish hedges, and 300 foot plus jagged black cliffs bordering the Atlantic Ocean. It's not a village as such, it's more of a collection of seven isolated, tiny hamlets: Crosstown; Woolley; Eastcott; Gooseham; Shop; West Youlstone; and Woodford are all accessible via long winding, narrow country lanes off the A39 Atlantic Highway.

Morwenstow was once the home of the eccentric parson and poet, R S Hawker (b.1803) he was the vicar there from 1834 until his death in 1875. He was a fascinating, larger than life character; much loved by his congregation. He disdained conformity and was, literally, a colourful character, known to wear swashbuckling leather boots up to his thighs, red trousers, a baggy fisherman's blue smock top, flowing yellow capes, crimson silk gloves, and wide-brimmed hats over his long untamed hair.

He was a large, sturdy looking man, and must have cut an impressive figure as he strode about his parish.

Hawker was credited with reviving the Harvest Festival custom, and wrote 'The Quest for the Sangraal' and 'The Song of the Western Men,' (aka Trelawny, which is now looked upon as the unofficial Cornish National Anthem.) His Morwenstow parishioners knew him simply as Parson Hawker, and his ghost, which is still occasionally sighted around Morwenstow, is still greeted by some locals in much the same way as he was addressed in life, but we'll get to that in the next chapter, 'The Bush Inn Haunting.'

When Hawker first arrived at Morwenstow he found a parish in severe neglect, materially and spiritually, and, as his biographer the Rev Sabine Baring Gould said: "He found dissenters of every hue." The church and the manse were in a deplorable condition, the church crumbling in disrepair, the manse housing 'beasts of the field,' and, as Hawker saw it, many of his new parishioners had become spiritually bankrupt, after spending many years with no parson to keep them in line! Leading by his own hard-working example, he began, from day one of his new ministry, to holistically address the needs of his new congregation. Most of that congregation eked out a meagre living, they only just had enough work in the spring and summer months, mostly labouring for local farmers, to keep their large families fed and sheltered, and during the winter months they were heavily reliant on a different kind of harvest, that which the sea had always provided.

The claim that the Cornish of old deliberately conspired together to lure ships to their dooms, in order to profit from their wrecks and jettisoned cargoes, is rightly debated. Wrecking was most likely a literary invention, but it made for a good story. Winston Graham and Daphne Du Maurier have, among many other writers, capitalized on it to great effect, whether they believed in its reality or not. However, in defense of Winston, in his Poldark novels, the leading character, Ross Poldark, is in a scene where he's in court defending himself, speaking to the jury, he makes it clear that on the day of the wreck, few people were on the beach with any lawless intent. He goes on to say that the idea of false lights luring ships to their doom, was a calumny spread by the ignorant and prejudiced.

There were more than enough natural shipwrecks for those in need of 'rich pickings' from the wild, dangerous Cornish coast, and particularly so on the north coast over any given winter; they didn't need to create any more. Consider that between 1824 and 1874, there were more than 80 shipwrecks along the coast between Padstow and Hartland. Hawker said, in 1870, "Along and beneath the southern trees, (in his church's graveyard) side by side, are the graves of between 30 and 40 seamen, hurled by the sea in shipwrecks, and gathered up and buried there." He went on to describe the sheer carnage on the Morwenstow coast after a storm:

"Limbs are cast ashore now and then, arms and legs, lumps of flesh, five out of every seven corpses have no heads, cut off by the jagged rocks, it is a fearful country to inhabit!"

Hawker's new parishioners, less than 300 people in total, had a long tradition of salvaging and free-trading (smuggling). Whatever goods 'God's Grace' had washed-up were always put to good use, for example clothing and food, and the ship's timbers would have been used for both shelter and warmth. Hawker saw their actions as ungodly and wanted to 'save their souls,' and so he had set about organizing working parties, to search the coast for shipwrecks and washed-up dead bodies after big storms. Hawker insisted that the men's first duty should always be to save lives, before taking any useful plunder. Hawker himself was responsible for retrieving at least 40 drowned seafarers, precariously carrying them up steep, dangerous cliffs, with the aid of ships' ropes, and giving them, after a specially devised funeral service, a proper Christian burial in the graveyard that overlooked the sea that had so cruelly taken their lives. Hawker also organized them to look for 'gobbets,' these were the remains of peoples' bodies, broken up in to small bits by sharp rocks that they had impacted during a shipwreck.

There were many tales of Hawker's good works in the district, it was said that his vicarage door was 'always open for the poor of his parish.' One Christian preacher and church historian of the 1920s claimed that Hawker was 'a Christian Communist.' He was also known to have had random psychic intuitions about his parishioners' needs, maybe they needed extra blankets, or perhaps food or medicine, and so, with his servant in tow, he would think nothing of rising from his warm bed on a foul night, to then walk some distance to their homes, to administer to their imagined needs; and his kindness and gifts were always well received, whether they needed them or 'no.'

Hawker also had a reputation, especially when he was younger, for playing practical jokes, and one of the best of these took place in Bude, a few miles west of Morwenstow, where he had pretended to be a Merry Maid (Mermaid). He had sat naked on a rock, except for a long flowing wig, and seaweed draped around his shoulders, for several nights running. The crowds had grown bigger and bigger every night as the word went around Bude that a Merry Maid was just off shore on the rocks. They turned out to watch her from the cliff-tops in their hundreds, but one night the Merry Maid failed to show up. Hawker had apparently caught a cold, and he had decided to give it a miss. His cold got better, but strangely that particular Merry Maid was never seen around Bude again. The children of Morwenstow absolutely loved Hawker too, he would sit them down in a circle, as the old Cornish droll tellers would have done in earlier times, and tell them stories of Cornish Piskies, Giants, Spriggans or the Knockers in the mines.

Rev R.S. Hawker

A Morwenstow Road-Trip

If you visit Morwenstow by road you will arrive via the A39 Atlantic Highway, head down towards Shop, and then take the signs towards Crosstown and St Morwenna Church. Before you get there you will see an ancient white-washed pub on your left, 'The Bush Inn', when you do, bear to your right and follow the road around towards the church, parts of which date back to Norman times. (Don't worry, we will return to the pub a little later for a ghost story, if not a beer.) As you head towards the church you will see, just on your right, before you get to it, Hawker's old vicarage with it's beautiful trees, stained glass windows, and elaborate, ornate chimneys. Opposite that church lies Rectory Farm, where in the summer months you can get a delicious Cornish cream tea.

Morwenstow Church has an aged, cool ambience, it's peaceful there, I like to say 'Hello' to Parson Hawker whenever I enter, and I have often felt his presence there. This may, or may not, be influenced by the large framed black and white photo of Hawker on the rear church wall; his eyes follow you everywhere!

It's always worth having a saunter around the graveyard while you're there too, you can read and learn about all the shipwrecks from the grave headstones, listen to the rooks' croaky chorus high up above you in the trees, and generally enjoy the tranquil atmosphere. Up close to the church lych gate you'll see the white figurehead from the Scottish Brig 'Caledonia,' which sank in 1842 off the perilous Higher Sharpnose Rocks, with only the one survivor. The Caledonian Captain and the rest of the crew are buried in the churchyard. In the late 1960s the female warrior figurehead disappeared from the graveyard one night, the police eventually recovered it three weeks later, in a field at Abottsham Cross, near Bideford. However, there was some minor damage to the figurehead, and a fund was soon set up to pay for her restoration. Hundreds of Scottish people visit Morwenstow every year to see that figurehead, as the ship had Scottish crew and families, and was built there too. The police, looking for the culprits, even pursued their enquiries up to the Scottish Arbroath area, but to no avail. Mr Jim Gregory, who was the landlord of the nearby Bush Inn at that time, told the police that if they were looking locally they were not going to find the culprits."Why would that be?" they had curiously replied, "Because local people would not be seen within a hundred yards of that figurehead at night!" Jim had responded, going on to explain there was an aura about the female figurehead that scared most people away. Hawker, it is now thought, began the rumours of the figurehead being haunted many decades earlier; it was a clever ruse to stop people vandalising or stealing the figurehead. Another local legend said that if you walked around the figurehead in an anti-clockwise direction thirteen times, the ghosts of the Scottish seamen would all rise up from the graveyard around you, and the feisty Scottish lass (the figurehead) would strike out at you with her sword!

I have my own theory as to why the figurehead of the female Scottish warrior was abandoned, very shortly after having been stolen. In more recent years we in the paranormal research world have become more aware that objects can have spiritual attachments. I would suggest that the spirits of the Caledonia crew members may have made a brief appearance in the thief's vehicle. If some 17th Century Scottish sailors had suddenly appeared in my car, and asked me to give a stolen item back, I too would have found the nearest field to throw it in, and got the hell out of Dodge, or, in this case, Cornwall!

The figurehead of the shipwrecked Caledonia, a feisty wee Scottish lass - you steal her at your peril!

Leaving the graveyard for now, take a side path on the field that leads between the farm and the church, and head alongside a Cornish hedge on your left, out towards the coastal path and the high cliff-edge. (It's a common suicide spot apparently, my dog, Geordie, was often aware of something sinister there, he was always in a rush to get away, ghosts of sailors and broken hearted people perhaps.) Turn left at the end of that path, preferably before you fall off the cliff and add to their number, cross over the Cornish stile, and then walk along the path in the Bude direction for a few moments, and that's where you'll find Hawker's famous cliff-top hut.

In 1844 Hawker cleverly cut the hut in to the cliff face, making it mostly from timber off the shipwreck of the unfortunate 'Alonzo.' The hut has stable doors on the front, a low wooden bench around the sides and rear, a granite slate floor, and the roof is covered in turf. Hawker himself salvaged those ship timbers, at great personal risk, as he dangled on the end of a heavy-duty rope over the cliff-side. When you sit in there, with the top stable-door opened out, you get a wonderful view of the Atlantic Ocean, and you're temporarily transported back to Hawker's time. Hawker enjoyed sitting in that hut for hours on end, reading, writing, and contemplating life, as he puffed away at his opium pipe. He would entertain illustrious visitors there too, people such as Alfred Lord Tennyson and Charles Kingsley, and it's quite possible that Hawker still pops by the hut from time to time, as I found out….

I visited Hawker's Hut a few years ago with my daughter, Natasha-Angharad, and we did some EVP (electronic voice phenomena) work. Having made sure first that we were totally alone in that quiet spot on the upper edge of the cliff-side. I prepared my Tascam recorder, and said, "Good morning Parson Hawker, are you with us here in your hut today?" When I played the recording back later, not expecting to hear anything except my own boring voice, we both heard a man's deep voice swiftly responding to my greeting, we think the voice said, "Good Morning." It was muffled and distant, and my question appeared to have been answered almost before I'd finished asking it, but that now makes more sense to me. (See my later chapter about the research of Joe Di Mare.)

The interior of Hawker's Hut is covered in graffiti, some of it is very old. The timbers are quite educational, I learnt that in 1913 'Bill loved Sally,' and, if memory serves, Sally also loved Jim, Arthur and George, and all in that same year, she must have been a very popular girl around Morwenstow. It is a tradition to carve your name somewhere on Hawker's Hut, but please do it as neatly as possible, and without obscuring previous signatories, and please, do try to keep it clean!

On your way out of Morwenstow, why not pop in to the haunted Bush Inn at Crosstown for a quick pint, or perhaps a cup of tea and a scone? The Bush Inn is the beautiful old pub that you passed on your left, shortly before you veered right to approach Morwenstow Church. If you are interested in the supernatural, and you clearly are as you are reading this book, you really shouldn't miss the opportunity, you never know what other-worldliness you might experience in that pub.

My young friend Harri grew up in Morwenstow, she spent a lot of time around the haunted pub; her dad was the Landlord. He still owns the pub, but now employs a manager to do the day to day business. Harri had quite a few odd things happen to her in and around the pub over the years, and, in the next chapter she'll tell you about the strangest of them all.

My now sadly departed friend, Michael Williams, investigated the Bush Inn many times, in the 60s and 70s, long before Harri and her family moved there, and he found it to be, as he said:

"One of the most haunted spots in the whole of the West Country."

Which is no mean feat given the stiff competition that the pub has throughout the rest of Cornwall, Devon, Somerset, Dorset, and Wiltshire.

Hawker's Hut, looking out over the Atlantic, here he entertained illustrious figures, wrote his poetry, and allegedly smoked opium too!

The Bush Inn Haunting

Chapter Thirteen

I first met Harri around ten years ago, shortly after my son Dexter befriended her at Barnstaple Music College, and I still have a lovely video of them performing together on a beautiful summer day in my Bude garden, from many years ago. More recently, Harri has made a few music videos around her Morwenstow childhood haunts; these can be seen on YouTube. Her music, which I highly recommend, can be found on the Vanilla Wax record label. I'll now hand you over to Harri, so she can tell you about her weird experience at the 13th Century pub:

"My father has owned the Bush Inn since I was a little girl. I'm twenty six now, but other than a few years that I spent in the Bristol area, where I did a music degree and performed my music, I have spent most of my life growing up around here, in and around Morwenstow and Bude.

It was about ten years ago that my dad first gave me the responsibility of helping to close the pub down at night, I would occasionally have to do this on my own. I had a few jobs to do, including cleaning the bars, tables, public toilets, mopping the granite flagstone floors, and turning off all the electrical appliances.

One night, whilst cleaning the granite floor slabs in the kitchen, I decided to take a break from my chores. I walked across the courtyard to the public bar to get a drink. I know for sure that I left my mop standing up in the bucket, which was half-filled with soap and water, and leaned up in a corner of the kitchen. That corner was secluded, you couldn't see that area without walking right around the wall that almost divided up the room.

After getting a drink from John, the bar manager, who had been closing down the bar for the night, I was on my way back across the courtyard to the kitchen, when I noticed, through the clear glass bullion panes on the door, the lights in the kitchen flicking randomly on and off. At first I just made an assumption that Judith, another member of staff, had gone in to the kitchen after I had left it, and must have been finishing off the mopping job for me, as I had seen her around the pub earlier in the evening. I opened the kitchen door, headed towards the area where I'd seen the lights flashing, to where I'd left my mop. As I approached closer I could clearly hear what sounded like somebody mopping, the sloshing of water, and swiping movements on the granite floor. I called out, "Judith? Is that you?" As soon as the words were out of my mouth, I heard, as if in response to my question, a loud metallic clanging coming from around the corner, and then, almost as if in slow motion, a small trickle of fast flowing soapy liquid ran out around the corner on the granite flagstones, headed straight towards my Doc Martens. I nervously laughed, still thinking that it might be Judith. I cheekily told her that she'd been drinking way too many vodka and lemons, but, just as I said it, I had reached the corner of the wall and looked around the other side, still expecting to see Judith stood there, but she wasn't, nobody was there! The galvanized mop-bucket was on the granite floor laying on its side, moving ever so slightly, with the bubbly, soapy water still trickling out. The thing that I immediately noticed, apart from there not being anybody there to have knocked it over, was that the mop itself was still standing neatly to attention in the corner of the room. If the bucket had fallen in a natural way, say, for example, that the mop handle had slipped down the corner of the room, then surely the mop should have been laying on the floor too. The mop had clearly been removed by someone, or something, before the bucket and it's watery contents had been violently turned over, and then the mop handle had been put neatly back against the corner of the room. There was evidence to support the sloshing wet mop-like sounds that I had heard, they were in the form of a large mysterious S shaped wet swipe on the granite floor; a spirit giving a little clue to their identity perhaps? I was confused, and maybe a little bit in shock too. It felt weird in there, I had suddenly felt quite cold and shivery. I wanted to get out of there quickly, and so I nervously returned back across the courtyard to the pub bar again. John was still there, but just about to leave. I shakily told him what had just happened. He said that Judith could not have been involved, as he had seen her leaving the pub much earlier that evening, and that he was the only other member of staff on duty so late. There was no way that John could have pulled a stunt like that on me, it just wasn't physically possible, given that I had left him in the pub to go back to the kitchen, and he would have had to have passed me to get there before I did.

John was disinterested at best, he suggested that I was tired, and that I must have dreamed the whole episode up. I walked away, reluctantly returning to the kitchen once more, to clear up the mess and finish off my chores. The kitchen still felt weird, the lights still flickering on and off. I told myself that it was probably due to old fashioned, faulty electrical wiring, and I tried to think of other things. I thought of music for new songs, and lyrics, but it was no use, I just kept getting the feeling that I was being watched; I was not alone. It was so eerie. I turned the radio on, and I turned the volume knob right up, really loud, just to try to take my mind off the odd events and hopefully scare away the unseen presence. After that mystifying experience, I never ever felt comfortable again anywhere around the pub, if I was on my own.

That same year, Sally, my mum's friend, who is very sensitive to spiritual energies, went up to the bedrooms above the pub bar area. She told us later that there was nothing currently haunting the pub, no residents as such, but, as it was once an active free-trade (smuggler's) pub, and because it was so old, spirits would always be coming and going, that they visit places that they knew and loved in their lives. That really freaked me out too, as at that time those ideas were quite new to me.

I recently had a conversation with some of our bed and breakfast guests at the Bush Inn. I asked them if they had enjoyed their stay, fully expecting an answer in the affirmative, as it's such a lovely old building in a quiet, beautiful area. They said that everything was lovely, except, that is, for the uninvited guest. I asked them what they had meant by that, and the lady explained they were kept awake for most of the night, by a large dark shadow of what looked like a man. Apparently the shadow had loomed over the top of the bed and the staircase in their room."

I'd like to publicly thank Harri for her highly credible witness account, and I wish her continued success with her music-making. Interestingly, although those bed and breakfast guests were not aware of this, the pub is known for the haunted staircase, where distinctive, creaking footsteps are often heard ascending and descending, but whoever is making those sounds is rarely actually seen as a full bodied apparition, only his shade it would seem. There was a minor fire at the Bush Inn in 1968, and several locals reported seeing a dark, shadowy figure, moving swiftly away from the burning pub. My favourite Bush Inn story involved an American visitor. The lady said that she saw an elderly sea-faring man, dressed in period clothing, who had apparently just suddenly materialized in her room. She haughtily challenged the man as to who he was, and what right he thought he had to be in her room, at which point he had curiously turned around to face her, and then just rudely turned his back, and walked away.......right through a solid wall!

My late friend, Michael Williams, was involved in a BBC Radio Cornwall series, entitled 'ghost Hunt' which visited the Bush Inn in 1986. As part of their investigation they set up microphones all around the pub, succeeding in picking up strange, unexplainable sounds on their tape recordings, most of which were recorded during the 5/6 am, and the 5/6 pm time slots. Those were the times that the 1980s landlord, Jim Gregory, and his wife, reported the most anomalous activities.

There have been numerous sightings of the ghost of the legendary Rev R S Hawker in and around the Bush Inn over the years. Many of the sightings of his ghost have been seen within just a few minutes' walk of the pub, in fact I wouldn't be at all surprised if the big, dark, shadowy figure, seen at the Bush Inn by Harri's bed and breakfast couple, and many others before them, was Hawker, as we know he was a big man given to wearing unconventional flowing clothing.

One elderly local lady claimed to have seen Hawker many times, she'd witnessed him sitting quietly in the church pews, and she had also seen him walking on the cliff-paths. Her attitude, as with other witnesses to Hawker's ghost, was never one of fear, she treated her many meetings with Parson Hawker as she would the meeting of a living friend, nodding her head to him in acknowledgement, and she claimed that he'd always touched his hat and smiled in return, clearly aware of her presence as he'd walked on by.

In 1975, a hundred years after Hawker's death, Michael Williams interviewed Constance Drummond of the nearby village of Stratton. Constance told him how she had been out walking on a quiet, rural footpath in Morwenstow with a friend and her retriever dog. They had both clearly heard heavy footsteps coming up swiftly behind. As they got to a corner they decided to stand back, and let whoever it was walking behind them pass. They noticed the dog flattening himself in to the hedge, shaking, in apparent fear of something. The footsteps got closer and louder, passed them by, and then gradually faded away, but with nobody to be seen.

Many people have no doubt that Hawker still walks the country footpaths around Morwenstow to this day. He is still seen in and around the church, the Bush Inn, and on and around the coastal paths. As one lady put it to Michael Williams, when questioned as to whether Hawker's ghost was still walking, "Oh yes, Parson Hawker often comes up here after morning service," as if it was the most normal thing in the world, and rather silly of Michael to even consider questioning it. It would seem that Parson Hawker still regularly visits his beloved Morwenstow and its parishioners 144 years after his death. Hawker, as you will have noticed, is not really thought of as a ghost by some local people, they tend to think of him as still being around the place, just one of the locals, and in some strange way, I believe he still may be.

The Bush Inn

The Ghosts of Poundstock Church

Chapter Fourteen

For our next story we will head south-west, down the A39 Atlantic Highway, by-passing Bude, driving on towards a small hamlet called Poundstock, it will take us about 25 minutes, but it's a lovely road with great views. St Winwaloe's (Poundstock) Church, is situated in a pretty wooded dell, between Widemouth Bay and Crackington Haven, but slightly inland, it has a fascinating and blood-thirsty history with plenty of ghost stories. Although the current church records at Poundstock only go back to the 14th century, there was a church recorded on the site in the Norman Domesday book of 1086.

There are several tales of outlaw priests presiding over Poundstock Church down through the years, preaching by day and doing illegal deeds by night, known to have been complicit in many crimes, including murder, highway robbery, piracy, free-trading, and one was even known to be a bit of a lothario, although it's perhaps unfair to mention him in the same category. Cornwall, like other remote parts of Britain at that time, would have had little in the way of a visible crime deterrent, and so it was a fairly lawless place by today's standards. The wealthiest and most violent people dominated Cornish society, gangs feuded over who controlled which areas and commodities.

In the hamlet of Poundstock, in the 1350s, there was a feud between the Penfound family, of which William, the assistant curate of the church, was a member, and the Beville family. It was thought that William Penfound had been in league with the Bevilles, in a life of crime, including robberies, piracy, and ransoming kidnapped wealthy travelers, but, at some point, for reasons unknown, they had fallen out. Events eventually came to a head when the Beville family came to Poundstock Church to attend Sunday service, on December the 27th, 1357, and, sadly for William and his family, it wasn't to pray, or sing the praises of their saviour.

William Penfound was doing his ecclesiastical duties, several members of his family were there with him at Sunday worship. Whatever had passed between the Penfound and Beville families, in the days and weeks leading up to that fateful Sunday, it had finally led to William being brutally hacked to death near the altar by members of the Beville family. It was said that blood splashed all over the altar and vestments, during the prolonged, malicious, attack. It is thought that William's family tried to intervene to help him, but were then also savagely murdered, in the same gruesome fashion.

It is believed that William Penfound's ghost was seen many times after that dreadful day, by many people. News of the awful crime soon reached London, and Edward III ordered a swift enquiry. John Beville was quickly arrested, and soon confessed. Other members of his family were soon brought to justice too. Despite clearly committing capital crimes, all of them were acquitted, although heavily fined, and some property seized by the English Crown. I wonder how much money changed hands to get them off the gallows. It must have been a sizeable amount. John Beville later recommended his life of crime, principally by continuing to kidnap wealthy targets travelling through Cornwall, and ransoming them. Maybe some powerful characters in London were taking their cuts, and perhaps also supplying tip-offs of wealthy people who were considering a journey through Cornwall.

Almost two hundred years later, in 1549, during the Anglo- Cornish War, aka the Prayer Book Rebellion, the vicar of Poundstock Church at that time, Simon Morton, was hung by the English from his own church tower.

It was a common practice by the English crown forces, as was destroying any Cornish churches that still clung on to the 'old Rome' religion. This is not the place to go in to the wider history of what was going on in Cornwall during those times, but let's just say that history is written by the winners. It's fair to say that the Cornish were treated by the English Crown in much the same way as the English rulers had treated the Irish.

A more recent ex-local priest at Poundstock Church, the Rev. Frederick William Marshall, told researcher Michael Williams that he had often felt he wasn't alone in the church whilst performing his duties. He regularly felt the presence of someone standing aside for him, so that he could go to the altar rail. Jane, one of Frederick's parishioners, said that she had been in the dimly-lit church one morning, sat in a pew praying, when she looked up and saw a priest at the altar rail, who she had at first assumed to be Frederick. Jane said that the priest was kneeling at the rail for much longer than he normally would have done, as he would usually have become aware of her presence, and stepped aside for her, so that she could speak to her creator in private. Hearing movement and footsteps, Jane looked up from her prayers, and she watched as 'Frederick' finally noticed her and moved aside, but Jane was then stunned to see the priest she thought was Frederick walk right through the church wall! William Penfound? Simon Morton? We will never know, but we can be confident it wasn't Frederick.

My friend Derek Thomas was visiting Poundstock Church, with his sister, one weekday afternoon, over twenty years ago. They were stood in the main entrance porch. The heavy inner door was closed but unlocked. Derek was aware that he could hear organ music coming from inside the church, and so he asked his sister if she could hear anything, "Organ music," she had replied. Derek quietly responded, "Yes, so do I," then opened up the wooden entrance door, and, as he had begun to walk inside, with his sister following in closely behind him, the music had inexplicably, instantly stopped. Derek and his sister, now very intrigued, walked immediately towards the church organ. When they got there they found that the keyboard lid was not only closed, but it was also padlocked and dusty, as if it hadn't been used for a long time.

The next day Derek returned to the church with his dad and his niece's husband, Roger, to have another look around the church. While they were there they met the vicar, who told Derek and Roger that he couldn't hang about for long, because he had to officiate at a wedding service soon. Derek mentioned his visit of the previous day, and how he and his sister had both heard the strange church organ music. Derek remembers the vicar had looked uncomfortable, and had responded in a terse manner, "I know nothing about it." Derek thought that if it had been some kind of piped music, the vicar would have just said so. However, the vicar did admit his wife had a ghostly experience in the church, but didn't elaborate on her experience, as he was so short of time.

On Derek's next visit to Poundstock Church, later that same year, he took Roger along with him once again. While they were there Derek borrowed Roger's mobile phone, he remembers it was a Nokia 35, and he took a few photos of Roger stood in various parts of the church. One of them, taken up by the altar where the murders of William Penfound and his family had taken place in 1357, showed significant orb activity, and another, which I have published here, clearly shows a small misty figure sat on the organist's bench, and, it seems to me, that whoever it is, they're looking at Roger! Having looked at the photo in more detail recently, I now believe there are other spirits in the picture too.

When the photo was taken, Derek and Roger had no idea that the apparition was there sat on the bench seat, and neither had they sensed any presences. Derek and Roger are both honest men, and would definitely not have faked any photographic images to fool people. Roger had only just bought his first computer system, he knew nothing of doing more sophisticated editing or enhancements, only how to take simple point and shoot pictures. It's a genuine photographic capture of a spirit, so the sceptics can harp on about CGI if they wish, as it did not exist in the mid to late 1990s when Derek took the photo.

This is the first time this picture has ever been published, and I thank Derek and Roger for that honour. Roger is the figure on the left with his head blanked out for privacy, but we are not so sure of the identity of the seated organist. Is it a little lady? We have to bear in mind that people, in general, were shorter a few hundred years ago, so it may have even been a man. There are plenty of suspects, judging by the gruesome history of Poundstock Church, a vicar hung by the English for not relinquishing his Latin service? A vicar, or member of his family, slain by a murderous mob? A vicar who likes to pop back to take communion from time to time? Maybe it's a long dead church organist who misses his organ playing days? Your guess is as good as mine.

The Legend of Bossiney Mound
Chapter Fifteen

From Poundstock Church we have headed about fifteen miles further down the A39 Atlantic Highway, towards the Tintagel area, but more specifically to a small hamlet called Bossiney. It is there that you will find, on the Boscastle to Tintagel coast road, the historic Bossiney Mound, an ancient earthwork. It is next door to Bossiney Methodist Chapel.

To look at Bossiney Mound now you would perhaps find it hard to believe that it played an important part in Cornwall's history, and is heavily featured in the Arthurian legends. My first conscious sighting of it came in November, 2012, when I was just across the road at the Bossiney House Hotel. I had been there for a sad occasion, a gathering of family and friends after a funeral service for a dear friend, Maurice, who had lived at nearby Tregatta. I recall looking out of the window on that depressing, bleak afternoon, at the unsightly, scruffy earthen hump, and wondering how it had got there, as it clearly didn't look natural. At that time I hadn't yet met Michael Williams - that was still four years in to my future - so I didn't know that Michael had bought the hotel back in early 1965, and had run it for several years before selling the business.

The Reverend Sabine Baring Gould was one of the West Country's many eccentric priests. He was also a novelist, and a folk story and song collector, but he was best known as the man who wrote the hymn, 'Onward Christian Soldiers.' He once said of Bossiney Mound:

"King Arthur's golden table lies deep in the earth under this earthen mound. Only on Mid-Summer night does it rise, and then the flash of light from it for a moment lights up the sky, before Arthur's golden table sinks back down in to the earth. At the end of the world it will come to the surface again, and it will be carried to Heaven, where the Saints will sit around it and eat, and Jesus Christ will serve them."

That was the piece that inspired Michael Williams' own Arthurian Quest at the mound, and the result of that quest would then kick-start his own investigations and writing about the supernatural, and shortly afterwards Michael would go on to set-up The Paranormal Investigations Group, of which, in 2016, I became a proud member.

Here's Michael telling his own story:

"My first supernatural encounter happened almost on our door step, for Bossiney Mound was no more than 200 yards from Bossiney House Hotel, which we owned and ran at that time. It is not a particularly photogenic spot, or a landmark likely to excite the average tourist. Gorse, ash, brambles, hemlock, and bracken are some of the ingredients which clothe this large earthen hump. The legend has it that King Arthur's Round Table lies buried beneath the mound, and that it comes to the surface on one night a year: Midnight on Midsummer Eve. On this particular Midsummer Eve I had been listening to the wireless, to a show called 'A Book at Bedtime,' and it had just finished. A few days earlier I had decided to put this Arthur legend to the test, but I asked myself was it really worth staying up a little later? The mound was no great distance away from the hotel, but I suspected I wouldn't actually see anything, but I thought I'd go over there anyway as it would give me, and Tex, our Jack Russell Terrier, some exercise and fresh air. It was 11:40 pm when I put Tex on his lead, there was no going back now, Tex was excited and pulling me towards the door!

When I got down in to the hotel reception area I was surprised to see three of our hotel guests. "May we please come with you to the mound Michael?" They asked. Earlier that evening I had told a party of six all about the mound legend, the other three of that six had already gone to bed. "Certainly," I had replied, but, in all honesty I was annoyed, it was something that I had wanted to do alone. I felt embarrassed as I walked across our gravel forecourt. I told myself that I was a fool for leading my guests, literally, up the garden path, and dooming them to disappointment. As we all strolled along, with Tex pulling away at our head, I made some feeble apology, preparing them all for the inevitable anti-climax I felt sure would follow, "These legends are all very well you know, but nothing ever really happens."

Soon the murky shapes of Bossiney Mound and the Methodist Chapel loomed large. There was no hint of a moon, and the wind was sending the slightest of shivers through the darkness. I felt refreshed now, but the presence of the trio still gnawed. At the end of Bossiney Lane I left the three of them to take a closer look at the chapel and mound, while I took Tex for a run. We agreed to link up a few minutes before midnight by the chapel and mound. Freed at last from his lead, Tex bounded away down the bumpy lane, a loose TV aerial rattled, and the volume of the sea increased as we moved closer to the cliffs. A light in one of the bungalows turned out, now there was only torch-light.

It was shortly after 11:50 pm when I got back to the top of the lane. There was no sign of the three guests, I guessed they would be somewhere near the chapel. I walked with Tex over towards the mound, and I asked myself, "Will the table rise from the mound tonight?" And then swiftly answered my own question, "Of course it won't." I stood by the mound, ruminating on its colourful history. It was once known simply as The Hill, a defensive earthwork used before they built the castle on the nearby cliffs at Tintagel. In later years, it was used as a gathering place for the locals, and it was from there, in 1584, that Sir Francis Drake, the conqueror of the Spanish Armada, had been returned to Westminster as a Member of Parliament by local Cornishmen. Bristol traders had also brought their slaves to this now rather unsightly ancient earthwork, to sell them to the local Cornish gentry.

But then it happened, the genesis of my interest in the supernatural, my historical contemplation was abruptly and rudely shattered. At precisely midnight, a light had suddenly appeared inside one of the chapel's windows. It glowed and was expanding, not at all like an electric light, more like a patch of moorland mist caught in a car's headlights, and soon it had covered two windows. How long that glowing light shone I'm not entirely sure, at least a minute, possibly even two. I was fascinated and had no sense of fear. As soon as the light went out I began to mentally search for explanations, considering reflections and passing traffic, but there had been none. At that point I was joined by three frightened figures, my guests, who were coming towards me from the little side road that climbs up to Camelford. They were excited. "Did you see that light Michael?" One asked. "Yes." I replied, "I did."

"So did we, we were by the chapel and we saw it come on and then go out." A second voice added, "It was more like a mist spreading than a light." I turned to the youngest one of the three, and I said to her, "Did you see it too?"

"Oh, no, Mr Williams." She had replied, "I was far too scared to look!"

We walked together closer to the chapel, I was still skeptical, despite the weirdness of what I had just witnessed with my own eyes. I was keen to take a closer inspection of the building. It was conceivable that somebody had been in there and turned a light on and off. But when we got there those thoughts were quickly dismissed, as there were no signs of life around the chapel.

Tex, who was always such a pugnacious dog, refused to go anywhere near the entrance door, he was tugging violently in the opposite direction, clearly sensing something that we didn't. I persisted, and, eventually, he slowly, grudgingly joined me. The door was bolted. We walked on, back towards the Tintagel to Boscastle Road. When Tex stopped to do his business, I peered back towards the chapel and the mound, but now there was only darkness, meanwhile, the three guests chatted excitedly about what we had just witnessed.

After breakfast the next morning, I popped down to the chapel and mound on my own to inspect the place in daylight, and the mystery just deepened. There were closed internal blinds on all of the chapel windows. That same afternoon, I conversed with our Bossiney House Hotel gardener, Jack Dymond, about what we had witnessed the previous night. He was a trustee of the chapel, and had a set of keys to show me around. Jack told me that nobody else could possibly have been in the chapel the previous night, as it hadn't been him, and only he had the set of keys to open the entry door, and the accompanying padlock.

I asked him all manner of questions to try and debunk what the three of us had witnessed, we went through every conceivable scenario to try to explain it away, but we just couldn't. Eventually, frustrated by the mystery, I asked Jack what his thoughts were on what we had witnessed. "You can't always find rational explanations for everything Michael, sometimes we just have to accept that man does not know the answers to everything."

The Methodist Chapel and Bossiney Mound

Ghost Vehicles of Bodmin Moor

Chapter Sixteen

The 284 mile long A30 Road currently starts its life slightly to the west of London, near Hounslow, and finally draws to a close near to Land's End, in the extreme west of Cornwall. There have been many changes to the entire A30 route down through the years, and many have been in my own life-time. The most scenic and remote stretch of the A3O, the bit that we are most concerned with for these stories, is the twenty two miles that straddle the lofty, mysterious, granite backbone of Bodmin Moor, between the ancient Cornish settlements of Bodmin and Launceston.

The moor itself stretches no more than twelve miles from north to south, and only eleven miles from east to west, but if you drive up there on a miserable winter's day, in deepest, darkest December, with your mind occupied by visions of Du Maurier's wreckers conspiring at nearby Jamaica Inn, I'll guarantee that you wouldn't want your car to break down, and you'll breathe a sigh of relief when you are finally down off the higher ground. In the spring, or summer, it is of course a totally different story, and you might find yourself searching for somewhere quiet to pull your car over, so that you can enjoy the spectacular, panoramic views. That's the thing about Cornwall, it's the dark and light.

In the 1950s a lorry driver and ex-merchant seaman, Patrick Humpherson, had an odd ghostly car sighting on the A30 Road between Bolventor and the hamlet of Five Lanes. This is Patrick's story, which I have borrowed from one of Michael Williams' excellent books, and slightly paraphrased. Please bear in mind when you read this that there were nowhere near as many vehicles on our British roads in the post Second World War years as there are now, and particularly so on the Cornish stretch of the old A30 near Jamaica Inn, where this event happened.

"My job was to deliver new vehicles from my employer's factories in Birmingham, Coventry and Oxford. On that particular night I was driving a new lorry from the Birmingham factory down to Falmouth on the South Cornish coast. It was a regular job for me, and I was very familiar with the route. By the time I had got to Five Lanes it would have been around 12:30 am. I really hadn't expected to see much traffic at that time of the night, or any signs of life, except perhaps for some straying cattle, which occasionally happened as I drove over Bodmin Moor. The road was steadily climbing up in to really dense fog, but with occasional clear patches. I hadn't been aware of anything on the road ahead of me, when, without any prior warning, a green car just suddenly came out of nowhere, and then passed me on my nearside!

I had no time to break or swerve, nor would I have had time to do so, as it was just there and then gone in a flash. But in those few brief seconds that I did see it, I took in a lot of detail, it was like an intense snap-shot image. It was an old green convertible, with the hood pulled right back. It had four young men occupants, all were singing boisterously, possibly drunkenly, and half-standing up on their seats. I recall one of the men, in the back, the furthest away from me, had his hat in his left hand. The car didn't have any headlights, the only light was that of an old brass oil lamp, fitted between the car's door and the windscreen.

I probably swore at those idiots for passing me on the wrong side, and I eased my speed right down, I was half-expecting another vehicle to emerge from the fog, but nothing did, and I drove on towards Falmouth, puzzled, but without any further untoward incident. The years passed by and I never forgot that night. I could never get the sight of that old green convertible car out of my mind. Strangely, looking back, I could recall no engine noise, but I did remember their happy singing. Another one of the four men, the one nearest to me, was wearing a three-quarter length brown tweed coat.

Rolling forward a few years now, I drove in to the bus and coach station by the Malakoff at St Ives. By that time I was driving passenger coaches for a living. I couldn't help but notice that John, one of my new work-mates, was on the receiving end of a lot of mickey taking from the other blokes, there was much hysterical laughter at the poor man's expense. Whatever it was about, John wouldn't back down, and kept trying to repeat his story.

After I parked up, I asked my mates what all the fuss was about. I was told that John had told them that he had encountered a ghost car the previous night on Bodmin Moor. I was, of course, very intrigued now, and had turned to John and asked him to tell me all about it. The other drivers by now had respectfully shut up. It turned out that John's experience had taken place just a few miles away from where I had my own ghostly car experience. Until that day I had always kept that strange experience to myself. But as John opened up to me about his experience, I realized that it was identical to my own creepy experience all those years earlier. The facts were exactly the same, the same old green convertible car, four young men, boisterous, drunken singing, the men all half-standing up as they passed by. I was stunned."

Michael Williams was speaking to a group of people in North Cornwall, on the subject of paranormal activity in the West Country. One of the audience told Michael how, only a few days earlier, he had been driving along a road near Bude, and had been aware of another car closely following behind him, but a few moments later, when he looked in to his driver's internal rear view mirror, there was now no sign of the car that had been following him, and there had been nowhere that it could possibly have left the road. The man was quite convinced that the car had simply vanished, and had expressed the view that a tiny percentage of the cars that we see travelling on our roads at any time may be ghost vehicles.

In October 2001, Michael Williams himself had a similar, brief, but vivid experience, on country lanes not far from his home at St Teath, on the edge of Bodmin Moor. He was driving back home when he had seen a grey van coming up the narrow country lane towards him. He halted his car at a suitable slightly wider spot to let the van pass, when, to his surprise, the van had just suddenly vanished! The manifestation had lasted probably less than half a minute, but he had no doubt about the reality of it. It was 4:30 pm, still light, and visibility had been excellent.

Perhaps the heavy presence of granite might play its part in these examples of disappearing vehicles, maybe somehow they are recording, and playing back, the last journey of somebody who was about to die at the wheel. Maybe, when we're in 'the zone,' by that I'm referring to that alpha wave brain state where we occasionally drive on automatic pilot, we are more likely to notice these odd events. We've all been there, our minds are temporarily like blank slates, similar to the condition that a good stage hypnotist can induce in people. We are then in the optimum position to receive a signal/broadcast of a fully charged, recorded traumatic event, that may have happened many years before.

Just recently, it came to my attention, whilst digging in to some research on Jamaica Inn, that two taxi drivers, on separate occasions, both of them whilst returning from South Wales to Cornwall in the early hours of the morning, had seen a phantom hitch-hiker on the A30 Road, somewhere between Bodmin and Launceston, fairly close to the turn off to Jamaica Inn. I have seen similar things elsewhere a few times over the years, I think it is fairly common, but most of us are too pre-occupied with where we are going to, and what we have to do when we get there, to really be present in the 'now,' and so we don't always notice when these inexplicable events occur.

Prudence Pepper and the Phantom Planes

Chapter Seventeen

We are staying up on the granite northern back-bone of Cornwall, Bodmin Moor, for the next few chapters, beginning with this strange tale. Before I tell you about Prudence Pepper's weird post-war experiences at Davidstow Airfield, I will first give you a little relevant background to her life before she arrived in Cornwall, and what led to the wartime events that paranormal activity appears to be replaying at Davidstow Airfield, some 74 years after the hostilities of the Second World War officially ceased.

Prudence had worked as an ambulance driver, and also as a motor-bike dispatch rider for the London Fire Brigade, during the Second World War. This was difficult, dangerous work that she did on behalf of her fellow Londoners, as London was frequently blitzed by the Luftwaffe throughout most of that time, and particularly so during 1940, when the rest of Europe had already capitulated to Nazi Germany, and Britain had bravely stood alone. Hitler, after getting a bloody nose from the RAF in the Battle of Britain, made the same mistake that Napoleon did many years earlier, he picked on Russia, and that decision was to ultimately cost him his demented dream of world domination.

Shortly after Britain had seen the Nazis off in the 1940 Battle of Britain air war over England, the USA and Canada had come to Britain's aid with man-power, munitions and money, helping to turn the tide against the Nazi war machine. Some of those brave Canadians and Americans who came over here to help Europe regain its freedom, were aircrew, members of various Allied military aviation forces, including the Royal Air Force

(RAF), the Royal Canadian Air Force (RCAF), the United States Army Air Force (USAAF), including the 93rd and 44th Bomber Groups, the United States Navy (USN), and others too, they all flew out of Davidstow at some point, and were involved in dangerous flight operations. Those operations included bombing German U-Boat ports in France, anti-submarine warfare, Atlantic convoy protection, and air-sea rescue work, and you can bet that they never had a dull moment. No wonder then that some of those brave deceased aircrew, and their planes, are still seen, or at the very least they are still heard over Davidstow, by those of us who are sensitive enough to tune-in.

Davidstow was, and still is, perhaps even more so now, a very bleak place. It is the highest airfield in the country, at 970 feet above sea level, and it was always prone to low cloud cover, which made taking off and landing extra difficult. The airfield was close to Cornwall's own 'twin peaks', Rough Tor and Brown Willy, and also the North Cornish coast. Aircrews operating out of Davidstow, as with many other British military airbases of the time, had a hell of a life during those war-time years, and many didn't survive. The last tenants of Davidstow Airfield were the RAF Regiment, a specialist RAF military police force. Soon after they left, in 1945, the British government finally shut the base down, the airfield was then abandoned for nature to reclaim.

Prudence at Davidstow

By 1959, just 14 years after the war had ended in Europe, and Davidstow Airfield had been abandoned, Britain began to settle down in to more peaceful times, after the awful strain and loss of life of those war years. Prudence, like so many of her generation who had endured such adversity, was mentally and physically worn out, she needed some fresh air and new surroundings to re-invigorate her, and so she had decided to finally escape the hectic hustle and bustle of London life, to go and live in Cornwall.

Prudence Pepper moved to a cottage about a mile from the village of Camelford, on the edge of Bodmin Moor in North Cornwall.

Prudence hadn't been living there for long when she first noticed that there were strange, unexplained noises in the dead of the night. A close friend and neighbour had also heard the noises. They agreed that the inexplicable sounds appeared to be coming from the direction of the nearby abandoned Davidstow Airfield, which they soon found out had officially ceased all operations in 1945. There had been some local rumours going around about phantom planes being seen and heard around the Davidstow base, and even witness accounts of stricken bombers trying to land. There had also been eerie reports of what sounded like huge explosions on the airfield ever since the end of the Second World War.

Throughout the early 1960s Prudence spent her free time investigating the now disused airfield buildings, and the strange nocturnal sounds. On her first night-time visit to the old airfield, arriving shortly before dusk on her trusty old motorcycle, she had hidden it away, as she was not yet sure who, or what, she might encounter up on the airfield. She made her way to the top of the abandoned air traffic control tower, which is, I can assure you, not easy in the dark, as it's hard enough during the day. I have visited the ATC tower, indeed, the whole airfield, with its disused buildings and air-raid shelters many times in the last few years, and it never fails to impress me, particularly so the wide-ranging view of the landing strips afforded by the vantage point where Prudence used to like to sit and watch. The visibility from the old watch tower was very clear on Prudence's first night time investigation, she had been able to see all around, easily making out the two main runways from the tower. She thought she might have fallen asleep at some point, but was rudely woken up by a loud rumbling sound, and strange droning noises which appeared to have come from above the old building where she was sitting.

An abandoned ATC building on Davidstow Airfield

Prudence had checked her watch, it was 3:30 am. The noise above her had been intermittent, but had got progressively louder. Prudence said the noises sounded just like aircraft coming in to land, but she had a great view of both runways, and there were no planes to be seen. She got the impression that the invisible planes were over-shooting the runway, and then trying to come around again. The problem for the aircraft, years earlier, had possibly been that the clouds were too low, and the instruments on the aircraft, giving the pilots their altitude readings, may have been damaged by enemy fire, and therefore the pilots didn't know where the ground was! Prudence heard a very loud swishing sound, swiftly followed by what sounded like rubber tyres skidding on the runway, and then the noise of a large explosion, or an impact, and it had come from the direction of the end of the runway. She stared down towards where the noise had come from, but could see nothing, except for briefly seeing an orange flare, and then nothing. Prudence had heard the sound of emergency vehicles arriving, and excited people shouting to each other, but, again, she couldn't actually see anybody, despite it being a very clear night. Prudence experienced the same noises, in exactly the same order, several more times that night, and then everything had abruptly just gone back to normal. When Prudence checked her watch, she realized that the whole repeating sequence of the swishing noise, the skidding tyres, the explosion, the orange flare, and the emergency vehicles and excited shouting always happened in no more than seven minutes.

Prudence left the old air traffic control tower in a bit of a daze that first night, she walked the runways for well over half an hour, looking for the evidence of what she had just heard, and of the flares too, but she had found nothing. No burning wreckage, no vehicles, no people, but there was, she thought, a smell of burning and fuel.

Prudence Pepper didn't stop in Cornwall, she eventually left her cottage on Bodmin Moor and returned to her family roots in London. Peter Underwood, once the president of the ghost Club, and famous for his 'Gazetteer of British Ghosts' book, was very interested in Prudence's story, having heard about it from his friend Michael Williams. The story goes that Peter tracked Prudence down to her London home a few years later, to interview her for one of his own books. He sat with her in her home, and asked her about the weird events of those dark, creepy nights out on Davidstow airfield so many years earlier. Prudence went through her story again for him, and he noted that the story was completely unchanged, that there was no elaboration from when she had told the story to Michael so many years earlier. Peter asked her if she would return to that desolate, deserted airfield during the early hours of the morning ever again. "Oh yes, I'd love to go back to that haunted airfield Peter, but at my age I can't run as fast as I used to, so I don't think I will."

I think there are two major factors as to why there is so much haunted activity at Davidstow Airfield. The first is that it sits on granite, which I discussed in 'The Granite Influence,' and the second is the turbulent history of the place (similar to the Stratton battlefield site) the extreme emotions that were played out on and around the airfield. For those who lived through those terrible war years, life was very hard, and of course, for those that didn't, it was often short and brutal. Allied aircrews had very short life expectancies, to survive at all was a miracle, given what they had to experience on a daily basis. For some of the brave aircrews that flew out of Davidstow it was perhaps the last place that they were alive on the surface of the earth. Davidstow was a hotbed of turbulent emotions, and somehow, and none of us yet really know how, or why, some of those final earthly moments are still being played out, seen or heard by those sensitive enough to get a playback. People like Prudence Pepper.

A Bristol Beaufighter, with its Canadian 404 Squadron Aircrew, at Davidstow.

The stripey (D-Day) markings on the fuselage were designed by a gentleman called Mr Goodwin, when he was serving in the RAF during the 1939/45 war. How do I know this? Because I lived next door to his lovely widow, Joyce, in Bude, for many years!

Jamaica Inn

Chapter Eighteen

You may have noticed that I have already mentioned Jamaica Inn in this book, but that should be no surprise really, as you can't discuss Cornwall's haunted legacy without mentioning Jamaica Inn at some point. So, please now join me for a metaphorical pint, or perhaps a cup of tea, at the renowned, and very haunted Jamaica Inn!

It is a public house/restaurant and hotel at Bolventor, just off the A30 arterial road on Bodmin Moor in North Cornwall, first made famous by Daphne Du Maurier's novel of the same name, and the Alfred Hitchcock critically acclaimed film of the book that followed in 1939. Daphne's initial inspiration for writing the novel had come from her first visit to Jamaica Inn in 1930. Daphne and her friend had been out on Bodmin Moor riding, when a heavy mist had suddenly descended on to the moor, quickly losing their bearings; they were soon hopelessly lost. The two ladies were frightened, scared they'd have to spend the night up on the exposed, bleak moor, and so they decided to trust their horses to lead them back to the Inn. They dismounted and, luckily for them, the horses instinctively lead the ladies back across the misty moor to the Inn. Daphne stayed a few more nights at the Inn after that chilling experience, recovering from her ordeal, and during that time she and her friend were entertained by the local vicar with scary tales of wrecking, highwaymen, smuggling and ghosts. That short but eventful stay at Jamaica Inn, nearly 90 years ago now, left its mark not only on Daphne, but also on everybody who has ever read the book, seen the films, or serialisations on the TV. Daphne was so affected by the haunting atmosphere of the Inn, and the bleak moors that surround it, that a compelling story, and strong characters had already begun to take shape in her mind. It was to be the genesis of one of the greatest novels of all time, the legendary 'Jamaica Inn.'

Daphne further researched Cornish history and learnt that there had been powerful, respectable figures in Cornish society who were, on the quiet, up to their necks in criminal enterprise. This had gone on for hundreds of years, as at Poundstock which we discussed earlier, but particularly so at Jamaica Inn, which was then a very busy equivalent to a modern day service station. Up until around the late 1800s, there were plenty of profitable crimes from which the unscrupulous could choose, including free-trading and highway robbery. The life-blood of their smuggling activities was heavy state imposed taxation, where commodities are banned, or heavily taxed, there are always big profits to be made. Some respectable members of Cornish society, such as local squires and vicars, were smart enough, like the Pengallan character in Daphne's 'Jamaica Inn,' to cash in on these crimes by orchestrating them from behind the scenes.

Jamaica Inn's haunted reputation is second to none. It was built in the mid-1700s to cater for travelers going east and west over the treacherous Bodmin Moor, between Launceston, the ancient capital of Cornwall, and Bodmin, the county town. It supplied weary travelers with food, drink, washing facilities, and a bed for the night, and, quite likely, ladies of the night too. In 1778, Jamaica Inn was extended to include a coach house, stables, and a tack room for the horses, which created the L-shaped part of the building as it stands today.

Jamaica Inn got its strange exotic sounding name as it was used by Cornish free-traders to hide away their contraband, mostly tea and rum, which they had bought in Jamaica, smuggling it in on the nearby Cornish coast, to avoid paying taxes. It is estimated that a quarter of all the tea, and half of the brandy being smuggled into Britain at that time, was landed on the Cornish and Devon coasts. The name Jamaica Inn also has strong connections to the local land-owning Trelawney family, as two of them were Governors of Jamaica in the 18th century.

Walter De La Mare once remarked of Cornwall:

"I don't feel safe again until I've crossed the Tamar, and left Cornwall behind."

Bodmin Moor could be a very dangerous place a couple of centuries ago, there were plenty of highwaymen preying on those travelling by horse and carriage on the rough, muddy road traversing the wild moor. It was not a place where you would want to hang around for long, and I'm sure that if you were travelling from Cornwall to the English side of the Tamar, west to east, you'd have been relieved when you were finally off that high granite backbone of Cornwall, and down in to more 'civilized' lush, green, territory.

Members of Jamaica Inn's staff, and its visitors, often remark that the busy, convivial atmosphere that they enjoy at the Inn during the day, totally changes as dusk approaches. I spoke to a lady member of staff a few months ago, in connection with this book, and she said much the same, before telling me of her own ghostly experiences, and those that others have had at the Inn. Some members of staff say that as the Inn quietens down for the night, there is a sense of the clocks having been put back by at least two hundred years, as a heavier, darker mood quickly descends upon the Inn, and the ghosts reclaim their old stamping ground.

So many people have seen ghosts at Jamaica Inn that it would probably take up less space here if I wrote about those who haven't experienced something strange there. My friend, the late supernatural researcher and author, Michael Williams, saw the ghost of a powerful dark character on four separate occasions at the Inn, in what was once called 'The Stable

Bar.' The phantom moved very quickly from the bar in the direction of the courtyard, and on each of those four occasions another witness had also seen the apparition. In October 1998, Michael and four other witnesses saw the ghost of a man sat on a bench in the small bar at the Inn. They were doing a quiet, 'dark' investigation session at the time. Michael told me that the man, who looked to belong to the early 1800s era, was not solid, but more like a faded watercolor painting of a man. When they turned the lights back on the man had not only vanished, but there was no bench there either.

One of the oldest stories associated with Jamaica Inn, from around the early 1800s, concerns a man, a stranger to the pub regulars of the time, perhaps a traveler, who had been enjoying a pint of beer at the bar. A loud male voice had been heard calling from outside by everybody in the bar. The stranger had seemed to recognize the voice, he put down his unfinished beer on the bar, then walked outside to the courtyard to meet the mystery man who had been hailing him. The stranger never came back in to the Inn to finish his beer, he was never seen again, well, not alive anyway. The next morning his body was discovered out on the bleak Bodmin Moor, he had been brutally murdered. The crime was never solved. Since that night, a man dressed in clothing of that era has regularly been spotted sitting on the wall outside the Inn drinking a beer, he never moves or speaks, and he vanishes when anybody, thinking he is merely a re-enactor or a local eccentric perhaps, approaches him. Maybe he is the murdered man, and he comes back to finish his beer, after all, tis a shame to waste good Cornish ale!

There are many ghosts at Jamaica Inn, and I suspect most of them are quite unaware of each other, as they may be haunting on different levels. The areas that have the most haunted reputation are the 'Smugglers' Bar,' the former 'Stable Bar' (which is now the museum) the old generator room (which is now the hotel reception area,) the original bedrooms,

'Pedlar's Restaurant,' the Gift Shop, and the stable's attic. There is talk of an American airman haunting the Inn too, apparently his plane had crashed on Bodmin Moor, and his body was brought to the Inn before being taken away by the local undertaker later. Many guests staying the night at Jamaica Inn, particularly those staying in rooms three, four, five and six, abscond in the night, preferring to take their chances out on the haunted, misty moor than stay in one of the Inn's many haunted bedrooms! There are numerous reports of footsteps walking up and down the corridors outside the guest bedrooms during the early hours, but when guests look in to the corridors, to see who it might be, there's never anybody there to be seen. There is also an odd looking man who wears a tricorne hat and a cloak, he likes to wake up guests, slowly walk past their bed, then walk through their wardrobe door, it's quite a party piece.

Many ex publicans, members of staff, and guests, down through the years, have heard prolonged conversations out in the courtyard spoken in what they usually describe as a foreign language or tongue. People out walking, and camping overnight, on nearby Rough Tor and Brown Willy, have also heard this foreign language being spoken around them when there's nobody around to be seen. I think it's safe to say that the language they hear is the old Cornish language, and maybe they are briefly experiencing a time-slip. Tony, a landlord of the 1990s, said that they could hear loud conversations and people shouting in the old Cornish language, and the sounds of horses and carriages being unloaded, which sometimes went on for at least two hours at a time, several times every year, but whenever they looked out in to the courtyard they could never see anybody there to account for the voices and sounds.

If ever, in a court of law, an example of a property was required by a judge, to try to convince him that granite somehow produces a field effect, enabling or increasing supernatural activity, then I would say to the judge, "I'd like to give you exhibit 'A' m'lud, Jamaica Inn."

Unearthly Screams on Bodmin Moor

Chapter Nineteen

In July, 1996, two young male campers thought they had found the perfect spot to pitch their tent for the night on Bodmin Moor. They were at the ancient Cheesewring stone circle on Stowes Hill, amongst the huge lumps of weather-worn exposed granite; once known locally as 'The Devil's Wring,' due in part to some of the rock formation resembling an old cheese press. There were local rumours too, that the massive rocks had once been used for the initiation of witches. One of those two male campers, James, wrote to Joan Amos at the 'Flying Saucer Review' to tell her, and her readers, their terrifying story. They had both just got off to sleep, in the early hours of the morning, when they had been rudely awakened by a very loud, hideous screaming sound, accompanied by a bright blue-white light that illuminated the entire Cheesewring area. They looked outside the tent and noticed that the intense light, and the awful screeching sound, were both coming from directly over their tent. The unnatural light was far too bright for the men to look at for more than a few seconds at a time, and, as quickly as the sound and light had arrived above them, it had disappeared, leaving the two young men in total blackness.

They were so terrorized by the sudden, unearthly, disturbance that they huddled together in their tent with a battery powered torch on, not daring to step outside again. Even when the torch batteries had finally ran out, they didn't let their guard down and try to sleep, so scared were they of whatever it was returning. They were petrified. When the morning had eventually come, tired and traumatised by their long, weird ordeal, one of the young men had nervously stepped outside the tent. Immediately screaming in horror at what he found; the grisly remains of a sheep. The front legs were missing, the spine contorted out of shape, the carcass lacking any flesh. Stranger still, there was no blood. The two young men were by now so freaked out by the whole scary experience that they hurriedly packed their tent and belongings away, and swiftly left the area.

A year earlier, also on Bodmin Moor and nearby, a man was driving, at around 10:20 pm, when he had noticed a group of weird lights ahead of him. The lights had appeared to be by the road side to his right. As he slowly approached them, he had seen a black triangular UFO, with red lights at each point, and at its centre. It travelled very low right over his approaching car (I won't say 'flew' as I don't believe these craft fly in the conventional sense). The totally silent black triangular craft was so low that the witness claimed he could have reached up and touched it. There have been many reports of similar UFOs all over the UK, it's worth checking out David Gillham's Cornwall UFO Research Group's archives, and the documentaries/meticulously researched investigative work of Richard D. Hall, on his 'Richplanet' website, if you are interested in learning more. I would also highly recommend the research work of David Cayton and Mike Freebury, who, like Richard, are also highly intelligent, honest, independent researchers.

The Cheesewring, on Stowes Hill

Ghosts of the King's Head Hotel

Chapter Twenty

We are staying up on Bodmin Moor for this chapter, and then we're going to head over to Newquay on the north coast for the next, but first you might, after that last scary chapter, fancy a pint, or perhaps even a strong brew of tea, well that's handy because we are now going to the King's Head Hotel, a very welcoming, lesser known old pub, just a short drive from Jamaica Inn. It's a wonderful place, very welcoming, with an open fire in the winter, it has great traditional locally sourced Cornish food, and proper Cornish beer, what's not to like?

The following accounts of an investigation at the King's Head Hotel, built in 1623, at Five Lanes, Altarnun, were kindly given to me by my friend Stephen Cleaves. Stephen, in his working life, is a Systems Engineer in the nuclear industry, but in his leisure time he is a long-standing member of the late Michael Williams' Paranormal Investigations Group, based here in Cornwall, which has, quite likely, been in existence longer than most other paranormal research groups in the UK. Here, in Stephen's own words, is his report of one of his many investigations at the King's Head Hotel.

"Over the years, I have visited The King's Head at Five Lanes, Altarnun, several times. It's a lovely, quintessential Cornish country pub, situated just off the main A30 Road. It serves traditional pub food along with many good ales and wines. I have spent many a fine evening enjoying their delicious food in front of their open log fire!

The landlady, and several members of staff, have reported various sightings of a fleeting dark figure in black, along with strange sounds in various parts of the premises, and some have seen objects being moved around, or even disappearing briefly, before re-appearing in a different part of the pub.

On two separate occasions I was staying at the King's Head overnight, with three other P I group members, carrying out investigations into the pub's supernatural activity. On the first occasion we placed audio-recording devices in to bedroom three (lots of strange activity gets reported by guests staying in room three), on the landing immediately outside that room, and also in bedrooms one and four. We all stayed up to around 1:00 am monitoring the devices, and also, of course, using our own senses too. Nothing was seen or heard by any of us, and so we all turned in for the night. The remainder of that night passed by without any further incident for any of us, and we all slept well.

Playing back our audio recordings the following day, the audio recorder in bedroom three had captured the distinct sounds of what appeared to be loud and clear footsteps walking around the room, although this particular bedroom is carpeted. The footstep sounds lasted for around six seconds in duration. Shortly after the footsteps, what sounded like a door latch being clicked open was heard, a very distinct and loud noise, but the door into that bedroom has a doorknob, not a latch. The other recording units did not pick up any similar sounds to the ones just described, but they did record sounds of more earthly activities during the night, such as members of our group coughing, and walking along the corridor to the bathroom. So, I wonder, why was the recording unit in bedroom three the only unit to pick up the footsteps and door latch sounds, whereas all the units, including bedroom three, captured the common sounds? This remains a mystery yet to be solved.

Our second visit to The King's Head was during May 2016. Since our previous visit the bedrooms had been substantially re-designed with the original four bedrooms now converted in to just three, and all of them ensuite and very well appointed. We only had two experiences that night; the first was a single chime of a bell, a few minutes after we had turned out the bedroom light. It had sounded like a bicycle bell, just a single chime/ping type of sound. My P I Group colleague reported that he felt a person, or something, sitting on the end of his bed about an hour later. It had felt so realistic that he had immediately switched on the bedside lights, expecting to see someone sitting there, but nobody else was present in the room. He didn't feel particularly perturbed by the incident, and the remainder of the night passed by quietly."

The following report was made by my late friend Michael Williams, the founder of the P I Group:

"The King's Head pub became a posting stage for coaches in the mid-1700s, and a local vicar once described it as an establishment frequented by smugglers and shadowy characters, where shadowy deals took place.' The King's Head has long had a haunted reputation. Peggy Bray, a long deceased former landlady, is reputed to take an occasion stroll around the place at night, and, more recently, a ghostly girl has been observed in the bar, seemingly real, only to suddenly disappear. Room three upstairs has an interesting reputation too, more than one visitor has heard inexplicable tapping on the outside of the bedroom window, and, on investigation, has found nobody there. I myself have felt unseen presences in this bedroom, and in the corridor outside."

Michael Williams' favourite pub, at Five Lanes, on the Moor

Cold War UFOs over Newquay

Chapter Twenty One

We've finally left Bodmin Moor behind us, and, like Walter De La Mare, you too may be relieved, as I know it can be a little bit unsettling up there. We are now heading over to Newquay on the north coast to get some bracing north coast sea air. It's a large, popular tourist destination, famous for its surfing beaches. I am very grateful to Michael, a member of David Gillham's CUFO Research Group, an ex-long serving police officer in the UK, for the following detailed account that he kindly allowed me to share with you. If I ever had to report a sighting of a UFO to the police, I would hope to get a policeman as professional, open-minded, and diligent as Michael. It's also worth considering that police officers are professionally trained observers, and perhaps also naturally inclined to be reliable recorders of information, or, to put it another way, they are what people in the UFO field like to refer to as 'reliable witnesses,' as they are also not generally inclined to flights of fancy.

The UFOs in the following account need to be put in to the context of the time in which they were observed, which was at the height of the Cold War. It was a time of very high tensions, and the ever present possibility of imminent nuclear war between the USA, its NATO allies, including of course us Brits, and the old Soviet Union. Cornwall has a strong American/British top secret military facilities presence, and perhaps that's at least part of the reason why the UFOs visit us so much. Many people have suggested that these visitors are not a threat to us, believing as they do that their interest in us may be out of concern for our warlike nature, and the destructive capabilities of our nuclear weapons. Why would that concern them? Well, it would affect their existence too, perhaps they are not from 'out there' at all, as is so regularly implied by the mainstream media, when they try to belittle those who have an interest in the subject. Perhaps, in reality, they are far closer than you might think, in a neighbouring dimension, or even co-existing with us in our oceans. (Check out the research of Preston Dennett). A nuclear conflagration would affect their lives too. Anyway, I'll get on with our story, and will hand you over to Michael, our retired policeman, to tell you that story, how he became involved with trying to help two young ladies find some closure to their UFO sighting.

"Back in the 1980s, I had already served at least ten years as a front-line, shift-working, uniformed police officer, when I was called out to see someone who wished to report the joint sighting of a UFO. The witnesses were two young women in their 20s. The older of the two informed me that her sister and she had both witnessed two UFOs whilst driving their car through Goonhavern, on the A3075 towards Newquay, near the north Cornish coast, at around noon on the day before, a weekday. It had been a bright, sunny day, and the skies, they informed me, had been clear, which had afforded them both excellent visibility of the aerial anomalies they witnessed.

The young ladies were both very trustworthy witnesses. I interviewed them separately, and they both related the exact same details. The UFOs had been headed in a north-westerly direction, and were at a height much lower than commercial airlines would usually take above North Cornwall. The two UFOs were travelling at quite a speed, much faster than the passenger flights that the ladies were familiar with seeing regularly passing over Cornwall. The UFOs they saw made no sound, nor left any contrails. They were quite large and had a silvery, reflective material appearance. The pair of UFOs had apparently travelled in-line, one after the other, and had no lights visible. The ladies made it clear to me that the UFOs were not of the usual saucer shape that was often reported by other witnesses to aerial anomalies. These they said, were more sausage shaped, and they appeared to have no wings or tail-plane. The ladies told me that they observed these two strange craft for several minutes, before they finally just disappeared in to the blue sky.

The young ladies took no photographs of the UFOs they witnessed, but back in those days, the early 1980s, most people did not carry around cameras, and mobile phones with cameras were still restricted to fantasy on TV's 'Star Trek.' I asked the two young women, again separately, to draw what they had seen. Their drawings both showed that the distance between the two strange aerial craft was approximately the same length as each of the craft, and that nothing appeared to be connecting the two UFOs together. I mentioned to the ladies that aircraft were occasionally re-fuelled in mid-air by military aircraft, and that sometimes a plane might tow a glider, but both young ladies were adamant that they were familiar with such things, and knew the difference.

After visiting the two women, and arriving back at the police station, I was determined to get to the bottom of this mystery on their behalf. I began to make my enquiries. Firstly, I rang RAF (Royal Air Force) St Mawgan, in the Newquay area, it's an air-base that at the time of the sighting, during the latter days of the Cold War, was also partly operated by the USAAF (United States Army Air Force). I faxed the drawings, and written descriptions of the two UFOs, to the St Mawgan duty officer. I received a response that St Mawgan had nothing flying in local airspace on that day, or at that time, to account for the strange looking silvery craft that the women had witnessed. I asked the officer if that would include any aircraft activity operating out of RAF Portreath, slightly further down the coast in Cornwall, and he replied that his response included all RAF and USAAF aircraft over-flying Cornwall, and, indeed, any commercial aircraft too.

My next enquiries were made to the RNAS (Royal Navy Air Service) on the south coast of Cornwall at Culdrose, and to the RN (Royal Navy) generally, to which I received similar negative responses. I then contacted the Coast-Guards at Pendennis Point, Falmouth, also on the south coast. The coast guards monitored vast tracts of ocean, but, once again, I only received negative responses to my inquiries. Next, I re-contacted RAF St Mawgan, and I asked them to confirm that there was definitely no air traffic from any of the smaller Cornish airfields which they might have over-looked. I was thinking of private airfields such as those at Perranporth, or other smaller airfields at Truro, Land's End or up on Bodmin Moor. Once again, I was told that they had all of the Cornish airspace covered by their radar, that no air traffic anywhere over or around Cornwall would go unnoticed by their state of the art equipment.

I was quite familiar with aircraft and their movements around Cornwall, for example, I knew that the big huge Nimrods flew out of St Mawgan, along with the old war-time Shackletons, plus they often had other RAF and NATO (North Atlantic Treaty Organisation) aircraft visiting the base. I knew too, that the RNAS at Culdrose, although it was best known by the Cornish public for its helicopters, also occasionally hosted various jets from other military forces. I decided to wait a few days, to see if any other local UFO sightings would come to my attention, or if I would read of any UFO reports in upcoming local newspapers, but it was all to no avail.

All the time this was going on I was also, of course, having to deal with other police business too, such as road traffic accident enquiries, and various local crimes. Ten days later I faxed my police log results of the UFO enquiries to the RAF, and the RN, for their records, I then informed the two lady witnesses of the negative outcome of all of my efforts. I heard no more from the RAF or RN after sending them my reports, although, I'd like to make it known, we did have an excellent working relationship with all branches of the military present in Cornwall, including the Americans that

Cornwall was hosting at that time. I have no doubt that had they known of anything that fitted the descriptions supplied to me by the two young ladies, they would have told me.

When I originally made my enquiries about these UFOs to the various military air-bases, I had never seen a UFO myself, but I had been aware of a UFO sighting in the north of England, following the well documented, reliable case of the alleged abduction of a fellow police officer, P.C. Alan Godfrey, in a UFO incident in November 1980."

The Merry Maids of Mawgan Porth

Chapter Twenty Two

This Merry Maid story occurred at Mawgan Porth, near Newquay, on the North Cornish coast, it was very big news in Cornwall during the summer of 1827, in fact the sightings made it in to the top selling Cornish newspaper of the time, 'The West Briton.' There is perhaps something of a clue in the place name that Mawgan Porth may have once been a place of regular Merry Maid activity; Mawgan is an old term for a Mermaid/man, the porth part means port or bay. A young local fisherman had been walking across a wide, sandy beach at low tide, to meet his friend. The lads had intended to do some pilchard fishing together when it got darker; and the light was already beginning to fade. As the boy walked across the beach he heard a weird voice calling out from a cave at the base of the cliffs. Smiling, he had assumed it to be his friend messing about in the cave, just being silly, trying to frighten him.

Now there were only two ways that you could get in to that cave, and both of them could only be accessed at low tide. The young fisherman decided to look in to the higher entrance to the cave first, which was well above beach level, assuming, of course, that his friend was in there, but slightly lower down. So he climbed up on to the rocks at the foot of the cliff face, and then peered down in to the cave below, but he couldn't see his friend.

The young man continued to look all around the murky darkness below him, trying to pick his friend out, but he could only see little pools of water, deep down inside the damp, echoing blackness, and hear water dripping in to the rock pools from great heights. He had then realized that there was somebody down there, or rather something, in that cave deep below him. The young fisherman's eyes were slowly becoming more accustomed to seeing in the poor light, enabling him to make out the shape of something large sat on a rock, on the sandy floor of the cave. It had at first appeared to be human-like, but it had then slowly occurred to him that it wasn't human, it was a Merry Maid, and she was staring right back at him through her long matted hair. The young man was so shocked by what he saw, that he didn't wait for his friend, he just ran all the way home. But our story does not end there.

The next morning three similar creatures appeared to three more witnesses, all of them men, who were walking up on Bre Pen Cliff. The newspaper report said the three witnesses were local people, and all were familiar with the sea, and creatures of the sea. The three witnesses told of how the larger Merry Maids were sleeping face down on the beach, and were human looking from the waist up. Their bodies, they had told the reporter, were coloured 'just like a Christian' (white I would assume, given the attitudes of the time) and their arms were like short fins. Their hair was at least nine feet long, the lower bodies blueish, and they had tails. As the Merry Maids slept on the beach, the three local witnesses could see the gentle swell of the incoming sea washing over them, and then receding, leaving them looking almost dry again. The younger, smaller Merry Maids were seen to be playfully swimming around the older, bigger Merry Maids.

On the following day, five more Merry Maids were spotted, also from up on Bre Pen Cliff. The witnesses, different men this time, apparently watched them for well over an hour. That's nine separate, reliable witnesses to the mermaids, over a three day period.

The Attempted Abduction of Cecil Morgan

Chapter Twenty Three

In Donald R Rawe's 'Cornish Hauntings and Happenings' he tells the true story of Cecil Morgan, a young man who had been out walking on the North Cornish cliffs with Susie, his spaniel, between Trevone and Padstow, in the 1920s. Cecil had stopped to admire the view out towards Harlyn Bay and Trevose Head. It was then that he had slowly become aware that all the natural sounds, that he would normally have expected to have heard whilst walking on a Cornish cliff-top, had suddenly, and inexplicably, just absented themselves. Sea-birds had taken flight elsewhere, and a dozen sheep, who were normally quite happy to just nibble the turf right up to the cliff's edge, had now all nervously huddled-up together, as far from those cliff-tops as they could possibly get. Cecil marveled at the eerie serenity of the weird unfolding scene, when he was made aware of subtle, dream-like, time-less sounds, emanating from the caves far below him. He later said it felt as if those strange sounds were emerging from some other plane of existence. At first, those weird sounds did not appear to be at all sinister, they had sounded almost heavenly, but as he became entranced by the music, Cecil soon felt a desperate urge to climb down the dangerous cliff-side, to the caves hundreds of feet below him, something he would not usually have been foolhardy enough to do. He knew something was luring him down there, he didn't know what that something was, but he knew he felt powerless to resist it. The sounds, Cecil later recounted, were more like soft, undulating sighs than singing, they were sighs of melancholic invitation, ethereal sounds that were way beyond our normal human comprehension, or capabilities.

Susie possibly saved Cecil from being a Mermaid abduction victim statistic that day, as she broke the spell that had such a powerful hold on him. Susie had suddenly appeared above him on the cliff-top, peering down past him as he was climbing precariously down. Cecil had shouted to Susie to join him, "Come on Susie, good girl, come on down!" Fortunately though, Susie was having none of it, somehow she had known better, Susie just stood there in complete silence, staring past him, not moving a muscle. Meanwhile, the weird sounds from the cave had increased in volume and urgency. Susie clearly hadn't wanted to join Cecil on his crazy quest, and Cecil had then been torn, should he keep going down, or should he climb back up the cliffs to his beloved spaniel Susie? Luckily for Cecil the power of love overpowered his illogical desire, and so he had climbed back up the cliff-side again to join her. Meanwhile, Susie had continued to stare angrily past him, down towards the caves, baring her teeth, mouth foaming, until Cecil finally reached her. It was only later that Cecil began to realize that Susie had known something, or perhaps seen something, that he hadn't, and that her intervention had saved him from an uncertain fate.

Cecil confided in a few local people later about his odd experience, one of them was a retired sea-farer, a Captain Crowle. The Captain told Cecil that he had experienced something very similar when he was around 14 years old. The old man recalled the sounds he had heard as being like a 'wordless chorale, like women's voices continually rising and falling.' Once again, with this witness account, we see the similarities to alleged alien abductions. The victims are aware that they are being pulled towards something, they know they don't want to go there, but they seem almost powerless to break the spell. I've read many alien abduction accounts where the victims report similar feelings. In Spielberg's 'Close Encounters of the Third Kind' film, three characters are drawn towards the secret UFO landing site by an all-consuming desire to get there at all costs, but they don't know why. I'm not suggesting that Mermaids are aliens, but I am saying look at the similarities. Many who have had strange experiences whilst sleeping, perhaps sleep paralysis, or believe they have been abducted, will understand that these Mermaid stories have similar qualities, that certain intangible otherness that can't quite be put in to adequate words. In the Greek myths they spoke of the Sirens having the 'voices of guilded lilies,' voices that were capable of entrancing and mesmerizing unsuspecting male victims. I think we are only just beginning to realize the enormous power that can be harnessed via sound frequencies.

Note: The name Morgan is derived from an ancient Celtic (Welsh/Breton) term (Morgens/Morgans/Mari-Morgans) for a malicious water spirit, or, to put it another way, a mermaid!

On the Cusp of a Paranormal Breakthrough
(Moving Beyond Belief)
Chapter Twenty Four

"I regard the existence of discarnate spirits as scientifically proved, and I no longer refer to the skeptic as having any right to speak on the subject. Any man who does not accept the existence of discarnate spirits, and the proof of it is either ignorant or a moral coward. I give him short shrift, and I do not propose any longer to argue with him on the supposition that he knows anything about the subject." –

James H. Hyslop

James Hyslop was a Professor of Ethics and Logic, and that confident, some would say premature and arrogant quote, is taken from his 1918 book, "Life after Death." It's 101 years later, and the sceptics are, understandably, still not convinced!

When I tell people that I write about the supernatural their eyes will occasionally roll, a response born of disinterest, or an ignorance of the depth of the data that is now available to serious paranormal researchers. We live in a world dominated by materialistic thinkers, materialism has been drummed in to us all from an early age by our institutions and mainstream media, but fortunately some of us still retain the ability to think for ourselves outside of the box.

Let's look at some of the people who are, even if only indirectly, in their own small ways, quietly working towards a better understanding of the paranormal, and ultimately, by so doing, the true nature of consciousness and reality too. There are creative deep thinkers in this paranormal field, but they are not well known like the more macho, ego-driven ghost show celebrities that tend to hog the paranormal headlines. These quiet, unassuming, dedicated people don't often get TV air-time, as they are perhaps not as charismatic as those that do, and therefore not so good at putting bums on seats, which of course is the name of the game, as it generates advertising revenue for mainstream TV stations. Many of these bright introverts are not the type to go looking for recognition in the mainstream, they're not so good at self-publicity, or maybe they just don't much care for it.

Joe Di Mare is one of those quieter, back-room, technical people, an intelligent guy from Nashville. I first met Joe in his home-town of Nashville, in January, 2017, thanks to a mutual friend, Adam, who had introduced us in Hermitage, Tennessee. Joe had heard about my upcoming visit, and had been keen to show me some new cutting-edge ghost hunting technology he was developing. To Joe's credit he hadn't wanted me to spread the word about his technology in order to make any money on it, all he had cared about was that other ghost hunters in the UK, and elsewhere, would get the opportunity to see what his adapted technology was enabling him to see.

Joe is a computer engineer/scientist for 'Big-E-Frame.' He has created real ghost imaging technology, which he calls 'Ghost Pro V.R.' Joe's been working on this technology since 2012, having cleverly adapted baby-monitoring technology, which had first been created by MIT, the highly regarded Massachusetts Institute of Technology.

Joe had been tipped off by a friend in a Tennessee ghost hunting group about MIT's technology. His friend had cleverly seen the great potential in it for ghost hunting. Joe told me that at first he was a little slow to check out his friend's tip-off, but had soon caught on to the possibilities, and embraced the challenges of adapting it.

Joe now works with that adapted technology on a popular ghost hunting show in the USA, 'Ghost Asylum.' The producers of the show, according to Joe, liked to play down the implications of his technology, wanting to keep the show anchored in the realms of entertainment. They perhaps felt that the wider TV audience were not ready to know that Joe's technology really does pick up on other beings, all around us, in other dimensions. Maybe, in more enlightened times, Joe will be revered for having been a far-sighted innovator, one of the people who had finally brought the paranormal in to mainstream respectability, by finally providing adequate proof, enough perhaps to even convince the hard-liner fundamentalist sceptics, that the things that we have been calling ghosts for hundreds of years, whatever they may be, really do exist. Whilst researching this chapter, I had another fascinating conversation with Joe. We were discussing ways in which we could communicate with these other intelligences, and Joe had introduced me to the concept of time dilation, explaining it like this:

"When you are standing at the side of the road, a car approaches you, and it whizzes past you, you try to have a conversation with the person in the car, but it's just not going to happen, unless we can find a way to bring our speeds closer together to communicate."

Electronic voice phenomena (EVPs) have a similar problem in that the voices are also faster, or slower than ours. Maybe, in other lighter dimensions, the inhabitants can wander in and out of our reality too, and pretty much undetected, but, with bright innovators like Joe around we will soon be able to see more of their comings and goings, in and out of our reality. One final word on Joe's Ghost Pro, for the skeptical, it's not computer animation, it's not a game, there is no trickery involved; this technology is for real.

In October, 2018, whilst attending David Gillham's excellent CUFORG's annual conference in Truro, I learnt a little about the research and experiments of the late Trevor James Constable, and Nik Hayes' more recent research and photography experimentation, which had been inspired by Trevor's earlier work. In a fascinating and occasionally amusing presentation, Nik told us how Trevor began his work in the Californian desert, in the 1950s, where he had devised ways to photograph what he considered to be UFO type objects that were invisible to our naked eyes. His work had revealed strange biological, fish-like life-forms, and craft which were disc-like in appearance; all traversing the skies in the infra-red part of the spectrum. Nik continues to experiment, his infra-red and infra-violet photography has captured thousands of strange images. As Nik says in his book 'The Invisibles':

"There exists an entire world around us that cannot be seen."

Joe and Nik are just two of our current cutting-edge paranormal researchers, but there are many other bright minds out there too, all beavering away, often alone, at their small pieces of the paranormal puzzle. Intelligent, dedicated individuals who are working on what I think of as the front-line, the pit face of supernatural research, at the most haunted, and, in some cases, the most scary locations. Talking of scary locations, I was just reading a book called 'Chasing Shadows' by a friend of mine, Larry Wilson. In the chapter entitled 'Williamsburg Hill' Larry tells of the night in 2010 when he, and his colleague Chris Mason, were investigating the Ridge Cemetery. Chris had just seen an odd soundless orange orb light, which had moved along the tree-line, almost as if preparing to land, when, a few minutes later, four to five jets had passed over, as if responding to their presence. Shortly afterwards, they had run into a teenager, and his aunt, who were also investigating the cemetery. They were both very excited, as they had also seen the weird light. They had described it the same way as Chris did, the teenager saying that it had looked fish-like, as if it was swimming in the sky. This is fascinating on two levels for me, the first being that the description of 'fish-like' entities corresponds with Nik's research in England, and the second, that jets had seemingly been scrambled to attempt interception, it appears to be standard military aviation practice to intercept/observe these unknown craft/entities. Our militaries, both in the UK and the USA, do appear to see these things on whatever state of the art tracking technologies they possess.

Larry Wilson is a friend of mine from Taylorville, Central Illinois. By day he works for the Illinois State Board of Education, but by night, and at weekends, Larry is a dedicated, fearless, paranormal investigator and researcher, for Urban Paranormal Investigations, a four man paranormal investigative team which he founded. Larry also makes films on paranormal and historical content, and writes fascinating books (see my Bibliography at the end of the book) on his investigations and research at haunted locations around the Mid-West, and further afield too. Among many other famous, and not so famous haunted sites, Larry has investigated Iowa's Villisca Ax Murder House several times, Missouri's notorious Morse Mill Hotel, and he continues to investigate local Illinois haunted sites too, such as the Ridge Cemetery at Williamsburg Hill. People will often tell you that ghosts are harmless, that there's nothing to fear but fear itself, and, largely, they may be correct, but it's not always true. I've personally had many supernatural experiences, I've seen a few ghosts in my time, of various kinds, and I've never yet been terrified, but I do know that my own father saw a terrifying apparition that temporarily rendered him speechless, and he was a big, tough bloke. Larry might not admit it, but he's a brave guy, he does most of his research on his own in haunted properties and graveyards. He has been attacked from behind by unseen forces, had stones thrown at him when he thought he was alone, but he never runs, and he always returns; the truth drives him on. I've seen a few of the on-site videos that Larry has recorded of strange anomalies, and his photos too, his work is truly cutting-edge, and well worth checking out. Larry, before working for the State, had worked as a private investigator, and a fair few of the skills that he learnt there have translated in to his paranormal research work; he also gives fascinating talks on his work, at paranormal meet-ups and conferences.

Then there are people who bring us all together to share our knowledge, some, like Carl Jones and Neil Geddes Ward, by arranging meet-ups, and others, like David Gillham and Adam Sayne, by organizing conferences, and yet more, like Jim Harold, Seriah Azkath, and George Noory, via their quality, intelligent paranormal podcasts and TV shows, they all help to bring the paranormal to a bigger audience and increase our respectability.

Most people who are not actively interested in the paranormal have no idea about the latest breakthroughs in our field, they judge us by the sillier paranormal shows on TV. They assume we all run around screaming every time there's an unexpected squeak in a dark building. They should try going on an investigation with somebody like Larry, they might change their mind. Those who have no knowledge, or any real interest in the paranormal, are quite unaware of the fresh evidence that new technology is beginning to supply. Many, I feel, would just rather not 'go there,' as the subject scares them, reminds them of their own mortality, or it challenges their long established set of core beliefs, it's that mainstream conditioning again. But for those of us who have seen ghosts, other anomalous beings, and strange unexplainable aerial craft, we can surely now move on from debating the paranormal at that low level, we can also discard that age old argument that we have always had with the sceptics, as to whether ghosts exist or not. Smart guys like Joe Di Mare, Nik Hayes, and Larry Wilson, have proved (to my satisfaction) that there definitely are unseen intelligences all around us. I don't need to wait for the acceptance of the mainstream media, or the approval of those who won't look at the evidence, we in the serious paranormal field should now move on, we should move 'beyond belief'......... the sceptics, and those with less experience and knowledge of the paranormal can catch up later, if and when they want to, or are ready.

Richard Lennie and His Night Vision Goggles

Chapter Twenty Five

A few miles south-west of Bristol, in the UK, at a small seaside town called Weston Super Mare, another paranormal innovator, investigator, and friend, is quietly just getting on with his own paranormal research. His name? Richard Lennie. Richard has always had an interest in the paranormal, but a few years ago, quite by chance, he heard an inspiring podcast interview with an American guest, Ed Grimsley.

Ed Grimsley, a native of the Arizona desert, sadly departed this life a few years ago. As a young boy Ed had regularly gone hunting with his father up in to the mountains, and it was during one of those early hunting trips that Ed saw something that had really grabbed his attention. At first, Ed had just presumed that he was seeing stars, but soon realized that these 'stars' were saucer shaped. They had raced down at tremendous speeds to far lower altitudes, stopped dead, tilted, and then emitted flashes of light, almost as if to say 'Hi' before zooming off again. Ed told how these craft had pulled some amazing stunts, maneuvers that even then, as a young boy, he had instinctively known could not have been performed by any existing human technology. That night, his father had already retired to his sleeping bag in the tent, and so Ed, being excited by what he had just seen, had gone in to the tent to wake him up, to get him to come outside quickly, to see the show. But Ed's father, when he did come out, had been somewhat underwhelmed by what had been exciting his son; he had seen it all so many times before. It was fairly unremarkable to anybody who lived in the area, and had ever taken the time to just look up in to the huge expanse of Arizona's clear night skies for a few minutes, unpolluted as they were by artificial light. Ed went on to say, how a few years later he had been out hunting with his father again, when he had, quite by chance, pointed his rifle upwards towards the skies, and had caught a quick glimpse of the stars through the telescopic sight on his rifle. Ed, his curiosity now aroused, had then searched the night skies with the rifle scope for the rest of the night. He claimed to have seen many UFOs moving around up there in the night sky, UFOs that when he looked away from his telescopic sight, he couldn't see; as they were only visible in the part of the spectrum that we as humans, with our naked eyes, are unable to see. Fascinated by what he was seeing through the 'scope, and knowing that the general public were largely unaware of what he had been lucky enough to witness, Ed had been inspired to research the availability of night vision binoculars/telescopes/goggles, intending not only to use them himself, but to also sell them to anybody else that wanted to share in his discovery.

Ed soon found that American military surplus night vision equipment was perfect for the job, as he began to regularly see UFOs in the night skies above his local area, these had included cigar shaped craft, some that looked similar to the beautiful Anglo-French Concorde, and small round craft, which he had estimated to be only about the size of a Mini-Cooper car. Ed worked his way through the different grades of night vision equipment available, known as 'generations.' Generation 1 was an entry level, and anything above that, generations 2 through to 7, were progressively capable of seeing further and further out in to space, and in much clearer detail too.

Richard Lennie, after an on-line chat with Ed, eventually decided to take a financial risk, and a giant leap of faith. He placed an order for some night vision equipment from Ed, opting for what he could afford to risk at the time; he went for generation 2 night vision goggles. Bear in mind that Richard didn't really know Ed at that time, Ed was just a stranger that he'd met on-line. Richard was taking a big chance that he could be wasting several hundred pounds, if the night vision equipment didn't follow through on Ed's amazing promises.

On receiving his night vision generation 2 goggles in the mail, Richard had hurriedly unpacked them, then excitedly awaited a suitably clear night sky to try them out (in England that could take some time). What happened next, or maybe I should say what eventually happened next, is a lesson to anybody who, like me, may be prone to being rather impatient at times! Richard used them night after night, frequently spending between three to four hours staring at the night skies through them (12 midnight until 3 to 4 am) but he never saw anything that he wouldn't have expected to have seen. Richard saw satellites, high altitude commercial airliners, stars (he saw lots of them) but did he actually see any UFOs, as promised by Ed on the phone? Errrrrmmm, well, no, he didn't. Richard was beginning to think that he had been duped out of a fair few hundred quid, by a smooth-talking American snake-oil conman. He was cheesed off, and he had considered giving up, putting it all down to experience, and probably unfriending Ed on Facebook too. Richard's neck and back were hurting from the long hours of looking up, his eyes were aching with the strain too; he was so fed-up with his complete lack of sightings. He was preparing to pack the night vision equipment away, to send it all back to Ed in Arizona, asking for a refund, or perhaps to just shove it all under his bed to gather dust, but Richard, to his credit, obviously being a far more patient man than me, decided to try the night vision goggles just one more time; and that one more time was to totally change his life.

The very next night, Richard saw three huge, and when I say huge, we are talking football pitch size huge, saucer shaped craft, directly over his head in Weston Super Mare. Richard couldn't believe what he was witnessing. He took his eyes away from the night vision goggles, rubbed them, then looked through the goggles again, yes, they really were still there, moving in a triangular formation. Just 15 minutes later, after the three huge craft had moved out of his night vision sight, he had seen another three massive saucer shaped craft headed north over his head, also in a triangular formation, but this time they were travelling much slower. UFOs, they're like buses, you wait hours and hours to catch one, and then six of them turn up all at once!

Richard has found, with experience, that the best time to see these craft, from the west country region of the UK, is between 12 midnight, and 03.00 am, but it may well be different elsewhere, dependent on your geographic location, the position of the Sun, and other considerations. For the skeptical, Richard does know a satellite when he see one, and he has seen hundreds in his time, he's not mistaking satellites for UFOs. Richard has noted, as have other witnesses to UFOs, that they appear to suddenly accelerate away in to the distance at unbelievable speeds, just like the fictional 'warp speed' of the USS Enterprise on TV's 'Star Trek,' and it's usually followed, about ten seconds later, by what looks similar to a big white flash of lightning. Richard thinks the flash may be the craft entering a gateway to another galaxy, a portal of some kind that we have yet to discover for ourselves. Speaking of 'Star Trek,' that 1960s TV institution, it's interesting how many of their fictional ideas have translated in to our modern lives, some 53 years after the show first aired, perhaps, as I believe, (check out my thoughts on Tulpas, in the 'Knockers' chapter in volume 2) we may even be capable of literally thinking things in to our reality, so beware of what you wish for, you just might get it.

Some people have asked Richard if they can use the night vision equipment during the day. Well, for obvious reasons, that's not so practical, but Richard does know of an Australian researcher who has perfected the use of old camcorder technology, in order to film UFOs which cannot be seen with the naked eye, during the day. The Australian researcher uses an infra-red filter screw-on attachment, sets the 'Zoom' control to 'infinity,' then pans out on to the blue sky. He regularly sees

UFOs through his equipment in that way, and when he does, he just presses 'record' to keep records of all of his sightings. Some researchers have even connected up their night vision equipment to a big cinema type screen, so others present can watch what his camcorder is seeing, live, or perhaps a second or two later. I have not yet purchased any night vision equipment, but I do intend to. I have attended many night sky watches in Cornwall and the US, just using my ageing eyes, but even I know the difference between satellites, space stations, shooting stars, and commercial airliners. I also know that it's very busy up there!

As a final thought, I was browsing the CUFORG Facebook page today, when I saw this comment from my trusted friend, and fellow witness to paranormal activities, Derek Thomas. Derek had recently taken the plunge too, he'd purchased some night vision binoculars, and this is what he had to say after his first proper night-sky watch:

"Hi everybody, I just tried out my new infra-red night vision binoculars properly, for the first time, and, oh boy, the skies were alive with strange anomalies! They weren't satellites, not commercial airliners either, god knows what I actually did see, but let's just say that there's stuff flying around everywhere up there! It's incredibly busy. Most of them were as bright as the stars, and moved with a definite intelligence and purpose. One of these anomalies went three-quarters of a circle around me, and others were really huge, there were also transparent ones, like fish-like life-forms perhaps, they were just drifting around, it was absolutely mind blowing!"

If you are interested in the night vision technology, it is currently still available on-line, but you'd best buy it quickly, as I'm half-expecting a disinformation campaign by the authorities to begin fairly soon now, as the interest in using NV spreads by word of mouth. The government/establishment don't want you to know about the life that is teeming up there. They will do what they can to tell the public that we are mistaken, they will wheel out the smarmy 'we know best' rent-a-sceptics, and TV 'scientists' to tell the NV people that they are only seeing satellites. It's what they do. They fear change, they fear losing control. Perhaps the sceptics of the claims of the night vision equipment users, and those who don't want us to know the truth should team up together. They could adopt these wonderful Billy Bragg lyrics, I think they would be fairly apt: "I saw two shooting stars last night, I wished on them, but they were only satellites, it's wrong to wish on space-hardware."

A Tribute to the Late Michael Williams

Part One

Chapter Twenty Six

Many of today's big names in the paranormal field, and their followers, know little about the extensive research of those who were studying this weird stuff when many of us were still in short trousers, outstanding researchers/investigators such as Professor Archie Roy, Maurice Grosse, Peter Underwood, Colin Wilson, and, yes, Michael Williams, who was every bit as talented as the previous four mentioned. Perhaps we in the paranormal field should occasionally cast our attention away from the thrill seeking, electronic gadget wielding, and demon-taunting TV ghost hunters, there was an interest in the supernatural long before they existed, and the old-timers can really teach us a thing or two if we seek out their work.

I was just thirteen when I first discovered Mr Williams' supernatural investigation books, beginning with his 'Supernatural in Cornwall', then moving on to many other titles over the next few years, including: 'Cornish Mysteries,' 'Superstition and Folklore,' 'Paranormal in the West Country,' and 'Supernatural Adventure,' but Mr Williams had far more arrows in his quiver. He was also a writer on the arts, music, literature, theatre and architecture. He was an independent publisher, an animal welfare benefactor and reformer, a hotelier, a talented cricketer, a sports enthusiast, and a Cornish Bard, amongst many other worthy talents, but for all that, due in part to his reserved, gentlemanly nature, he was little known outside of his native Cornwall.

Many years would pass before, quite by chance, in around 2014, I would find myself living just a few miles away from Mr Williams' home in North Cornwall. I wrote to him asking for permission to do an interview in relation to this series of books. In the letter I explained how he had been a great influence on me since the early 1970s, with his books on ghosts and other strange goings-on in Cornwall. Michael graciously allowed me to interview him a couple of weeks later, it turned out to be a fascinating afternoon, and the beginning of a fond friendship. It was also the day that Michael cut me short when I addressed him as 'Mr Williams' one time too many, "Please Mark, call me Michael, we are friends now!" Much of the information I received from Mr Williams, sorry, Michael, that day has found its way in to these books in one way or another.

A few years later, in 2018, I was attending a meeting of Michael's Paranormal Investigation Group in the King's Head Hotel, at Five Lanes, on Bodmin Moor. Several weeks earlier I had sent Michael some of my fledgling writing for this book, to look over and critique with his knowledgeable, more educated, experienced eyes, and I had cheekily requested if he would honour me by providing a Foreword for my book. I hadn't heard anything back for a long time, but a few days before the PI Group hotel meeting and lunch, our mutual friend, Elaine, his secretary and close friend, sent me this very brief message:

"Hi Mark,

Michael will talk to you about your writing at the meeting.

Regards,

Elaine."

I wasn't sure what to expect from Michael, but I had wondered if he hadn't been too impressed by my writing, and might say, "Sorry Mark, no," to my request. After the morning session with the group, I had walked through from the bar area to the restaurant, in order to prepare for lunch. Michael and Elaine had laid out little name tags at all of the tables, to show members and guests where he wanted them to sit. Michael liked to do that, so we could all get to know each other better, and because it encouraged the swapping of supernatural experiences, stories and ideas. I searched hard for my name card, and it took me rather a long time to find. The name tags were small, and written in slightly shaky free-hand by Michael. When I finally located my seat at the table I was a little taken aback with emotion, the card had simply read:

"Mark Anthony Wyatt, Writer"

Those extra six letters that Michael had written after my name, coming from a man of his stature, a respected, published writer, a true gentleman who had inspired my interest in the supernatural many decades earlier, had sold thousands of his books worldwide since the mid-seventies, and had been happy to spend some of his private time guiding my fledgling writing career, meant the world to me. We all seek, in our various fields of endeavour, validation and acknowledgement from those who have already made the grade, that we belong too, and it had felt as if Michael was holding out a literary baton for me to take, just as he had been passed that baton, inspired, and guided by his own creative mentors in his younger days. Thank you Michael.

A Tribute to the Late Michael Williams, Part Two

"My great hope is that before very many years have passed, we shall see a major breakthrough in the supernatural field. The reality of ghosts will be established, and, on the evidence of the past, there's a very good chance that the breakthrough will be made here, in Cornwall." - Michael Williams, speaking in 1996.

Author's note:

I'm not quite as confident as Michael that a major paranormal breakthrough will actually be made here in tiny Cornwall, but I do hope, that in some small way, my ramblings and musings here in this book series will influence a reader to someday push things forward, to help create that breakthrough that Michael was hoping for, wherever in the world it might occur.

The Cornish people, via their pioneering ingenuity on steam power (which went on to fuel the industrial revolution) and the export of their mining/engineering skills and experience, have helped to shape the modern world that we all live in. I sincerely hope that by writing this book I have helped to draw some favourable attention to Cornwall. For such a small region they have had a hugely disproportionate positive effect on the world. The paranormal may only be a minority interest, but I also hope that this series of books will help in some small way to push things forward too, and, if nothing else, at least my friend, the late Michael Williams, may finally get the wider recognition from the paranormal community that he should have received in life. I hope so.

'Supernatural in Cornwall' the first Michael Williams' book title I ever bought, from a newsagent in St Ives, in 1974.

Bibliography

The following, in no particular order, are some of the books that I have gone to for my research, and have inspired me to produce 'The Spirit of Cornwall: A Haunted Legacy' volumes 1 and 2, there were many other books too, and no doubt I'll remember them after these books have been published, but in any case I highly recommend them all!

The Science Delusion, Rupert Sheldrake, 2012

The Sea is in the Kitchen, Denys Val Baker, 1962

Killers on the Moor, Mike Freebury, 2011

The Lost Gardens of Heligan, Tim Smit, 2000

Hawker of Morwenstow, Piers Brendon, 2011

Cornish Shipwrecks, the North Coast, Clive Carter, 1970

Voyage into Cornwall's Past, Nigel Tangye, 1978

The Call of Cornwall, Frank Baker, 1976

The Spirit of Cornwall, Denys Val Baker, 1980

Folk in Cornwall, Rupert White, 2015

The Wreck at Sharpnose Point, Jeremy Seal, 2003

The Sun and the Serpent, Hamish Miller and Paul Broadhurst, 1989

The Story of Cornwall, A.K. Hamilton Jenkin, 1942

Ghosts of Cornwall, Peter Underwood, 1983

Cornish Hauntings and Happenings, Donald R. Rawe, 1984

Dimensions, a Casebook of Alien Contact, 1988, and Passport to Magonia, 1969, Jacques Vallee

The Warminster Mystery, Arthur Shuttlewood, 1967

Popular Romances of the West of England, Robert Hunt, 1871,

The Occult, 1971, and Mysteries, 1978, both by Colin Wilson

Ghosts in Cornwall, Eric Hirth, 1986

Footprints of Former Men in Far Cornwall, R. S. Hawker

Jamaica Inn, Daphne Du Maurier, 1936

All of the Poldark novels, and Poldark ' s Cornwall, Winston Graham, 1945 to 2002

Alfred Wallis: Primitive, Sven Berlin, 1949

Vanishing Cornwall, Daphne Du Maurier, 1967

Chasing Shadows, Larry Wilson, 2014

Many titles by Brad Steiger, 1965 to 2017

Many Titles by Dennis Wheatley, 1933 to 1977

The A303, Highway to the Sun, Tom Fort, 2012

Many Titles by W.B. Herbert, 1980s

Traditions and Hearth-side Stories of West Cornwall, William Bottrell, 1870/3

Strange Things in the Woods/More Strange Things in the Woods/ and My Strange World, all by Steve Stockton, 2015/18

Davidstow Airfield and Cornwall at War, Stephen and Sheila Perry, 2013

RAF Davidstow Moor, 1942 to 1945, a Wartime History, Rod and Anne Knight, 2013

Abduction: Human Encounters with Aliens, Prof. John E. Mack, 1994

Valis, P. K. Dick, 1981

Human Race Get Off Your Knees: The Lion Sleeps No More, David Icke, 2010

The Messengers: Owls, Synchronicity, and the UFO Abductee, 2015, and Stories From the Messengers: Owls, UFOs, and a Deeper Reality, 2018, both by Mike Clelland

Communion, Whitley Streiber, 1987

Silver State Monsters, David Weatherly and Lyle Blackburn, 2019

J.B. Priestley, his 'time-plays,' 1930/40s

Glastonbury, Dion Fortune

The Hurdy Gurdy Man, Donovan

Knights of the Road, Gypsy Dave Mills

The Coat of Many Colours, Sven Berlin

Britain's Art Colony by the Sea, Denys Val Baker

The Tregerthen Horror, Paul Newman

The Timeless Land, Denys Val Baker

My Cornwall, by several prominent Cornish associated writers, including Michael Williams, Daphne Du Maurier, Jack Clemo and Denys Val Baker, 1973

The Way to the Minack, Derek and Jean Tangye, 1968

Haunted Cornwall: Supernatural Stories, Edited by Denys Val Baker, 1980

Crosbie Garstin, The Penhale Trilogy, 1920s

Quest for the Invisibles, Nik Hayes, 2016

The Supernatural in Cornwall, and many other books by Michael Williams, early 1970s for over four decades!

Legend Land, the Great Western Railway publicity department, 1922

The Cornish Review (various issues) Edited By Denys Val Baker, 1943/74

Acknowledgements

I would like to thank all of the following people for helping me out on this two volume book project, either directly, or indirectly.

My Dad, for had he not met a ghoulish gunpowder factory worker back in the early 1960s, I may not have become so fascinated by the supernatural, and, ultimately, wouldn't have written 'The Spirit of Cornwall: A Haunted Legacy.'

Janice Louise, a fellow paranormal enthusiast, you have helped me to create this book by kindly giving me the benefits of your editing skills, and, despite being an American, having far superior knowledge of punctuation and grammar. You have shared your fascinating paranormal research, prior knowledge, and thoughtful advice, and kept me supplied with endless coffee, meals and snacks. You have put up with my snarkiness, as the long hours and hard mental graft of writing, and researching, have occasionally got the better of me. You are a beautiful lady in so many ways, and this book would not have been published without your help, guidance and encouragement. Thank you x

My three lovely kids: *Natasha, Dexter and Bradley*, I love you all, and I'll always be proud of you xxx

Ali, for giving me three wonderful kids, and so many happy years when we were all younger. You will always have a special place in my heart x

My Irish American friend*, Bill*, a pluralist, animist, artist, member of the Thursday Night Club (which meets every Wednesday, ha, ha!) and haiku poet, for opening my mind to the ramblings of philosophers, and kindly allowing me to use a couple of his own musings in these books. Bill encouraged me to continue to write in my own authentic English voice, and not to adopt American ways. I have not known Bill for very long, around three years, but I count him as one of my favourite people; and I'm proud of the 8 per cent Irish ancestry that we share!

The rest of 'The Thursday Night Club,' *Linn, Paula, Jeff, and Denise* (of Cornish ancestry) for reading my first book (Wyatt's Weird World) and giving me such great feedback, encouragement and praise; I hope that you will all enjoy these books too.

Maurice Willmott, my old friend who passed on back in 2014, an Englishman by birth; a Cornishman by nature. He encouraged me to write my first book when he said: 'Get your bloody finger out, and just do it!' I hope that, wherever he is now, he will be pleased that I finally did get my bloody finger out. I miss you mate, you lit up every room you ever walked in to.

My friend, the late *Michael Williams*, a life-long inspiration. Thank you for allowing me to quote a few stories from your many books, for your friendship and patience, and for the lovely Foreword that you wrote for this book, which I'll always treasure.

David Gillham, a good friend of mine for many years now, the founder of the Cornwall UFO Research Group, for being so generous in giving me, with the permission of his sources, such interesting information to share in this book. Thanks to his lovely wife Elaine too, for putting up with me kidnapping her husband to talk about UFOs in his man-shed, and for her many years of hard work helping David to organise his excellent conferences.

David Lea, for helping David Gillham to organise his CUFORG Conferences, you do an amazing job Dave!

Derek Thomas, my old Black Country pal, with a voice deeper than a Cornish tin mine shaft, for sharing your experiences, and for being so supportive. You're a diamond mate!

Extra special thanks are due to *Max Faulkner, Helen, and Big Wave Dave*, who read through the Grenville chapter and gave me their blessings to publish, provided that I corrected a few small but important personal details, which I did. I'd also like to acknowledge that I used an excellent drawing for the 'Skatman' chapter that was not my intellectual property, I have no idea who drew it. I found the drawing in the attic at Grenville, when I was helping to save Skatman's belongings. All of his personal effects, including that drawing, would have ended up in a skip, had it not been for Niall Wilson, Dexter Wyatt, and myself. I passed those personal effects on to Max. I did try to trace the artist, but with no luck. Please make yourself known if you recognise it, so I can either credit your name to the drawing, or omit it in any future editions of the book, it's your choice.

All the past residents of Grenville Gate, far too many to list, but you know who you are!

Adam, Robbie, Serfiel and Luke of the *Conspirinormal Podcast*, for allowing me to waffle on, and on, about my research, my writing, and even my musical tastes on their show. Thank you too for being such welcoming hosts whenever we visit Nashville, and for the kind invitation to talk at your inaugural conference.

Steve Cleaves, a longtime member of Michael William's Paranormal Investigations Group, and a knowledgeable, experienced paranormal investigator in his own right, for allowing me permission to publish some of his Cornish paranormal experiences/investigations.

Elaine Beckton, one of Michael Williams' best friends, also the secretary of his Paranormal Investigations Group. Elaine was always so kind and helpful to me in my communications with Michael.

Matt James: Thanks for the leads you gave me to witnesses to strange events in Cornwall, and for your own odd experiences too. I value your friendship, intelligence, and quick wit, and look forward to attending more night sky-watches with you on Cornwall's granite hills and coastline; hopefully we won't get lost next time.

My new friends *Shelly and Bella*, of the excellent *Weird, Wacky, Wonderful Stories Podcast,* for having me as a guest on your show. The WWW stories are always interesting, and I love the unforced humour too, keep up the good work!

All the other paranormal podcast hosts, and radio stations, who have invited me on to their shows in the last few years. I can't recall all of them now, but, from memory, thank you Jim Harold, Jimmy Church, Paul Eno, Seriah Azkath, Adam Sayne, Steve Stockton, Sysco Murdoch, Sean Kneese, Brent Raynes, Neil Geddes Ward, Tom Warrington and any other hosts I have temporarily forgotten, it is much appreciated, and maybe we can do it again sometime soon.

I'd like to thank all the witnesses/experiencers of paranormal activities who I haven't yet mentioned, they include:

Rob and Niall Wilson
Len and Lydia Dell
Harri Tape
Mark Hobbs
JC Stell
Verity Perkins

Adrian Nicholas
Matthew P Delaforce
Bryony and Joe
Alex Anderson
Kevin James
MJ Michael
Tom Dell
Derek Thomas
Debbie
Graham Towse

I wish to thank the following people for their inspiration, quotes I've borrowed, or for just helping me out along the way:

Winston Graham
Denys Val Baker
Colin Wilson
The Rev RS Hawker
Daphne Du Maurier
Charles Dickens
Peter Underwood
Donald R Rawe
PK Dick
Rupert White
Jeremy Seal
Thomas Hardy
Sven Berlin
Piers Brendon
Eric Hirth
Lucy Jenkins
Colin Silbert
Dennis Hill
Tom Fort

Clive Carter

Kay Walsh

Glenys Berson

Hamish Miller

Paul Broadhurst

Christopher Knowles

Bob Dylan

Donovan Leitch

Tim Buckley

Rod and Anne Knight

Steve and Sheila Perry

Tim Smit

John Nelson

Cousin Jacks and Jennies all over the World

The Pobel Vean

Cornwall's Merry Maids

The Rev Lionel Fanthorpe

William Bottrell

John Lane

HH Price

WB Herbert

AK Hamilton-Jenkin

Frank Baker

Crosbie Garstin

Rupert Sheldrake

David Icke

Dean I. Radin

Rosemary Ellen Guiley

Richard Lennie

Matt, Menna and Margaret

Neil Geddes-Ward

Richard D Hall

Mike Freebury

David Cayton

James Sweet

James McEwan

Nigel Moyle

Dan Younger

Scott Marshall

Dave Sweet

Russell Brown

Jo Ball

Danny Ball

Huggy

The Wizard of the West

Bob Boyd/Plymouth UFO Group

All the lads and lasses who were at Bude Royal Mail when I was there (2005/7)

Jacques Vallee

John Keel

John E Mack

Algernon Blackwood

Arthur Shuttlewood

Carl Jones (thanks for the opportunity you gave me to talk about this book at Praireland Paranormal Consortium)

Larry Wilson (thanks for your publishing advice)

David Weatherly

Seriah Azkath

Tom Warrington

Brent Raynes

Sean Kneese

Paul Eno

Steve Stockton (for your inspiration)
Maddy Hilker
Archie Roy
William Woollard
Jim Harold
Brad Steiger
Joe Di Mare
Trevor James Constable
Nik Hayes
Kyle and Cameron
David Paulides
Sysco Murdoch
Whitley Streiber
Mike Clelland
Gypsy Dave Mills
Albert Romiel
Paul Newman
Dion Fortune
George Knapp
George Noory
Jimmy Church
Christopher Erickson
Wharton Lang
Danny, Sophie, and Dan Allen Snr
Malcolm Ian Wyatt (Writer and big little brother!)
My Cornish Family in St Ives, past and present
Grenville Gate
The Tinners Arms, Zennor
The Tree Inn, Stratton
The Kings Head Hotel, Five Lanes, Altarnun
The Kings Arms, Stratton

Jamaica Inn, Altarnun
Tregenna Castle Hotel, St Ives
The Bush Inn, Morwenstow
Life's a Beach Café, Bude
The Davidstow Airfield and Cornwall at War Museum
and Uncle Tom Cobley and all…..

The author, looking out over St Ives Bay.

Author's Contact Details

Mark Anthony Wyatt may be contacted via his e-mail at markanthonywyattwriter@outlook.com

If you, or somebody you know, has encountered something weird or inexplicable in Cornwall, please contact Mark and let him know about the experience, and you may, if it is your wish, find your experience in a follow-up book.

Mark is available to discuss his books on any reputable podcasts, radio stations, or TV shows. He's also available to give talks on paranormal topics, selected local history, and creativity in Cornwall, to small groups, or at conferences. His books are available from Amazon, Waterstones, Barnes and Noble, and various other quality book shops and online stores.

"When discussing supernatural research, the risk of talking apparent nonsense has to be taken, and I predict that in the future, the hesitancy of intellectuals to acknowledge such ideas will become a source of amusement."

— *Professor H.H. Price*

Cornish flag of St Piran

Kernow Bys Vyken!

PREVIEW, 'The Spirit of Cornwall: A Haunted Legacy' (Volume Two):

If you have enjoyed this first volume of 'The Spirit of Cornwall: A Haunted Legacy,' then please read the second volume too! The second volume concentrates on the western half of Cornwall, but it also has a series of interesting essays on various paranormal topics.

Mark Anthony Wyatt

About the Author

Mark Anthony Wyatt

Born into a haunted, historic, creepy, derelict gunpowder works in the Tillingbourne Valley of South Eastern England, Mark first cut his paranormal teeth on his dad's traumatic ghostly encounter on the site, thereby setting the stage for his own later other-worldly experiences, and a life-long interest in the paranormal.

Mark's widely-varied life experiences, including his first trip down to Cornwall in 1973, were some of the stepping stones that led to him writing 'Wyatt's Weird World,' and 'The Spirit of Cornwall: A Haunted Legacy,' volumes one and two. Late in to his 50s now, Mark loves to research, write, and speak on topics that are of interest to him. He recently (2019) added a new arrow to his quiver, by delivering a well-received talk at the 'Strange Realities' Conference, in Nashville, Tennessee.

"In fond memory of our friend Uggie"

Made in the USA
Lexington, KY
07 November 2019